Kenya Interlude

Some Memories

John Parker

Cressar Publications, Ludgvan,
Cornwall TR20 8XG

Cressar Publications,
Ludgvan,
Penzance, Cornwall
TR20 8XG
UK

Printed and bound in Great Britain by Book Printing UK

ISBN 978-0-9535399-4-9

Distributed by York Publishing Services, 64 Hallfield Road, Layerthorpe, York. YO31 7ZQ

Kenya Interlude
Some Memories

John Parker was for five years a teacher, teacher trainer, and educational administrator in the 1950's in pre-independence Kenya, working in African schools and colleges.. In this book he reproduces some of the black-and-white photographs he took then, as a record of his work and of his leisure activities such as the ascent of Kilimanjaro as leader of a multi-racial group of young people. He attempts to show how primary school teachers especially battled against parental apathy and shortage of funds in trying to bring as many children as possible into the school system. He seeks to convey through the photographs the great love he came to have for the people and landscape of Kenya, and his devotion to the aspirations of the African people with whom he worked. It is also an account of a country on the verge of independence, full of hope for a prosperous and democratic future.

Contents

In memoriam
Eve and John Byrne

KENYA

I spent five years of my life, from 1953 to 1958, working in Kenya Colony and Protectorate as it was then, as an officer in the Education Department, and during that time I took a number of photographs on a small vest-pocket Kodak camera which I had bought cheap at an auction. After my return to England I decided to write a travel book illustrated by these same photographs, which were in black and white for the simple reason that colour film did not become available until around 1958, when I was in my last months in the colony. This book would be, in my opinion at the time, and that opinion has not changed since, a candidate for the worst illustrated travel book ever written, so awful and uninteresting were the pictures. However I began putting the book together, describing each picture in my best chancery hand which I had recently learned if not mastered. I so liked the resulting look of the handwritten page that I have used a similar font, "Lucida Calligraphy", in this presentation.

The pictures accompany some sort of narrative, taking the reader through my stay in three different places, Nyeri, Nakuru and Kitui, where I spent the greater part of my time. My final posting was to the African Boys High School in Machakos, but I have no relevant photographs of my time there.

In addition to my commentary on the photographs I took, I have included two reports on school visits and an account of my ascent on two occasions of Kilimanjaro, all of which I wrote at the time. I have also included a list of words borrowed into English from local languages, mostly from Swahili, the language of the Coast Arabs and the *lingua franca* of East Africa; words which one heard spoken every day by fellow Europeans, and which enriched and gave a unique flavour to conversation, and which have never had any place in the English of the British Isles. Most Europeans picked up a little Swahili in addition to these words, often limited to the version known as Kitchen Swahili, spoken by British housewives to their servants. I heard a friend make a brave attempt at translating "Don't clean everywhere, just the dirty bits", which emerged as "*Hapana safisha* everywhere, just the *chafu* bits".

As a government officer, I was required to learn Swahili and to pass an examination in the language. I began studying Swahili at the School of Oriental and African Studies when I was training in London as a teacher destined for East Africa, and I passed the standard examination within my first year in Kenya. I also squeezed my way through the standard examination in Kikamba, the language spoken in Kitui, the incentive being a bonus of £50 for a local tribal language learned during one's first tour of duty. I couldn't actually converse in the language but I knew just enough phrases to qualify, and my written Kikamba was passable.

My memories of my time in Kenya are mixed. Certainly I fell in love with the country and within two years had decided I wished to spend the rest of my life there, although it was not to be. I got on very well with the Africans I worked with, and made some very good friends among Europeans and Africans alike, but being a bad correspondent I let nearly all of these friendships slip when I returned to England. On the other hand I suffered occasional frustrations in my work which took a little of the gilt off the gingerbread, mostly through lack of funds which hampered my work in the field, but this has always been a common problem anywhere in the world of education. I believe I did the best I could in the interests of my students and of the schools and teachers for whom I was responsible. My last enterprise before I left Kenya was to produce a staging of Shakespeare's "Henry the Fifth" with my final year students at Machakos (it was their set book for the Oxford examinations) and they did me proud.

Kenya will have changed a lot since I was last there, and I have never had the heart to go back. Even before I left, lines of electricity pylons were marching across the Rift Valley and so I prefer to keep my memories of this beloved country as it was when these photographs were taken.

NYERI

As I have already said, in 1953 I was appointed *via* the Colonial Office to be an Education Officer with the government of Kenya. My first posting in August of that year was to Kagumo Teacher Training College near Nyeri in Central Province, just south of Mount Kenya, where I almost immediately became temporary Head of Maths. I remained at Kagumo until February 1955 when I was posted to Nakuru as District Education Officer.

Most of the photos I took in Nyeri were intended to let my family at home know where I was living and what the countryside was like. The photographs seem to be mostly lacking in human content, for reasons which I can't remember. However, here is one which survived, showing the Principal of the college, Dick Lockhart, and his wife; Tom Preston and his wife Ethel and their three children; and at the rear, me, all standing in front of the Lockharts' bungalow.

At first I lodged with a colleague, "Robbie" Roberts and his wife Rae, but then I was able to "borrow" a bungalow normally occupied by a colleague who had gone on leave. I hired a "house-boy" called Kanini, a local Kikuyu, who was my housekeeper and valet, and a cook we called simply "Mpishi", the Swahili for "cook". Kanini was the epitome of efficiency, an African "Jeeves", and I very much missed him when I was posted away from Nyeri.

When I first came to Nyeri, the Mau-Mau – call them what you will – were active in the area and the compound which contained the college was surrounded by barbed-wire and patrolled by armed police at night. In order to strengthen our defences, some of the younger European staff were invited to become temporary policemen and I was recruited into the local Kenya Police Reserve. I was given a uniform (picture on right) and a 0.303 rifle, whose use I had mastered during my National Service in the R.A.F. For some months I carried this rifle everywhere and usually left it in the classroom at the end of a lesson, when my students would kindly remind me: "Mr. Parker, your gun!".

While at Kagumo, in between teaching and supervising teaching practice, I helped run the college Scout troop. We had uniforms, and staves cut from a bamboo thicket growing in the grounds. We cut wattle trunks to use as poles for bridge-building, and although we never slept out in tents, we practised camp cookery. The picture on the left shows maize porridge being cooked on a traditional fire in a sufuria, with a second sufuria on top.

I also ran a Scout troop at the local European primary school (up to age 13) and a self-imposed task for this troop was to keep tidy the grave of Lord Baden-Powell, the founder of the Scout movement, who retired to live in Nyeri and who is buried with his wife in Nyeri cemetery. Their grave is now a national monument.

There now follow some pages about my time in Nyeri.

This is the first place in Kenya which I could call my own, to the extent that I felt empowered to burn off the lawn as an alternative to having it cut. (As soon as the rains came, it burgeoned a beautiful green.) The Land Rover was the first car I owned and for nearly four years it was my pride and joy. It would turn practically on a sixpence ("thumuni" in local currency) and it had a delightful gearbox which would operate without the mediation of the clutch, as long as the revs were correct. For the benefit of those with poor vision, the registration number is KBF 721, the K standing for "Kenya". The trees are blue gum and had a permanent carpet of dead, crisp leaves around them, which did at least mean that one flank was protected against surprise attacks by Mau-Mau terrorists. It looks as if I have a plank strapped alongside the car; this is quite likely, as I had (indeed have always had) a propensity for carrying planks around with a view to carpentry. This may have been a plank of camphor wood, a wood which releases the most beautiful smell when cut. On one side of the bungalow is a warning S.O.S. rocket in case of terrorist attack: it was worked by a button from inside the house. Neither rocket nor button is visible here.

This, as far as I can recall, is the only photograph I ever took of Mount Kenya, the great rugged and eroded volcanic peak which dominated not only the town of Nyeri, near which this picture was taken, but the whole of Kikuyuland. Moreover the Kikuyu name "Kirinyaga" of the mountain was corrupted by the British into "Kenya" and so gave the name to the whole colony. This magnificent mountain can not quite be seen in the original photograph as a faint shape on the skyline, with banners of cloud streaming from its upper slopes. Why is it that I can't photograph mountains? (On the other hand, see my splendid likeness of Kilimanjaro elsewhere.) My only consolation here is that one can get a good impression of what was for Kenya a very good road surface. Note the loose stones and the corrugations in the surface. Now and then a "grader" in the shape of a bulldozer would come along and scrape the surface smooth and level. The wayside foliage was brown with dust. If you persisted in following this road far enough, you fetched up in Naro Moru.

A view across the playing fields of what was in 1954 the European Primary School in Nyeri, which taught children between the ages of 7 and 12 and provided boarding accommodation for children from farms within a fifty-mile radius. Dominating the whole school, indeed the whole town, was Nyeri Hill, reduced by the mechanics of my camera to the beforested pimple in the background. It was said that the summit was occupied by Mau-Mau but I never had the occasion to check this assertion. The trees with the feathery (O.K., pinnate) leaves are maybe jacaranda, the tree with the celestial blue flower (but celestial is too weak a term to describe the sight of an avenue of jacaranda in flower, especially since the flowers precede the leaves and so have nothing to hide them from full view). The low hedge may have been kai-apple thorn; it looks adequately prickly. The huts beyond the trees are not the school buildings. No need to mention that the day was as perfect with regard to weather as you could wish.

The term "multiple store" is hardly strong enough to describe the Aladdin's cave which lies behind the modest windows of the shop of Osman Allu and Co., Ltd., in Nyeri. Operated on the same principles as Selfridges or Harrods, it supplied almost anything you might desire in a few hundred square feet of floor and shelf space. Beer, buttons, fishing tackle, French perfumes, clothes and cigarettes inside; motor oil and tyres outside. Osman himself (fisherman and poet) occasionally appeared; the store was run by his numerous family connexions. They would send out for anything not kept on the premises, such as milk and meat: they would send for other things to Nairobi or Durban or London, if by any long chance they did not have what you wanted in stock. (In another shop in Kitui I asked for French mustard; the owner obligingly sent to France and obtained a jar of English mustard labelled "Moutarde Colman" which I accepted without comment beyond profuse thanks.) Nearly every European living within twenty miles was a customer with a monthly account, or at least an account. The soldier striding along on the right is doubtless also going in for picture postcards or snuff or something; the askari (tribal policeman) in the pillbox hat and long coat is studying the adverts. The naked-looking gari on the left with the carrier bag belonged to me.

One fine morning I awoke in my bedroom (last window on the right in the earlier photograph of my bungalow) and felt a paralysing pain in my right side, just forward of the kidney. I was obviously close to death so I drank my tea, shaved, dressed, cancelled breakfast and all my teaching engagements for the day, and drove five miles into Nyeri in my Land Rover KBF 721. I was admitted with a temperature of 95° to the European hospital, here depicted in its entirety, and was discharged thence three days later having survived an acute attack of indigestion. During this time I shared a ward with a old boy who had been driven 200 miles in a lorry from the Northern Frontier with a slipped disk, and who told me comical naval stories to while away the time. One concerned an admiral who, already a KBE, was then made a KCB. A colleague telegraphed him: "Congratulations – twice a (k)night – and at your age." Another concerned the captain of a cruiser who found that the heads suffered damage whenever the guns were fired. He begged to be excused from firing until the cause could be ascertained, but his admiral told him to fire as per instructions. He did so and then sent the following message : "Exercise performed as instructed – shit-house shattered as anticipated."

On a later occasion I attended as an out-patient here for an ailment which may be described concisely as "boils on the bottom" and which required a course of injections administered by a rather attractive young nurse. Nonetheless, all rather unglamorous, especially from my end (the bottom end).

While I was at Kagumo Teacher Training College, Nyeri, an African colleague of mine, (whose name I forget) was married, and I was invited to the wedding, along with my friend Robbie. After we had been sitting in the little Mission church for about an hour or so, the bride arrived and the ceremony was carried through. The church lay side by side with the mission's primary school, shown here; both buildings were constructed of mud plastered on to a wattle framework, and were roofed with flattened four-gallon paraffin cans—"debbies" or "debes" or more correctly (conforming to Swahili grammar) "madebe". The wattle framework is clearly visible in this somewhat "Oxfammy" picture. The wedding reception was held in the first classroom (the nearest door in the photograph). The guests' raincoats (it was the wet season) can be seen draped across the window-sill. The guests (not visible) are draped across the desks in the classroom. The shiny patches on the roof are new tiles, not yet gone rusty.

On our way back from the wedding mentioned previously, Robbie and I stopped, for some reason now forgotten, at this quiet spot. (The new bride and bridegroom had a less tranquil start to their honeymoon: their car was caught in cross-fire between tribal police and terrorists, and they spent an uneasy few minutes on their tummies under the car.) The drunken-looking trees are black wattle, an import from Australia and very fast-growing, ready for cutting seven years after planting. It is a basic part of the economy: its wood gives timber for building and for firewood (kuni) and also for powering the railway engines of the time; its bark is rich in tannin, and, when green, can be split into strips and used as lashings for the fences of the region, such as you can see here. Just below the fence is the road, though you don't <u>have</u> to believe that. A lump visible near the river may be the small boy who came down and washed himself very thoroughly while we were there: on the other hand it may be just another tree stump in Kikuyuland.

RHINOCEROS

Well, here I was, and about twenty feet away from me was a great big White Rhinoceros. He (or she?) appeared to be quite unconcerned by my presence, and the definition of the detail in the picture suggests that my hand was quite steady, and that this feeling of unconcern was mutual. My own sensation of security was based largely on the presence between us of a ditch, seven foot wide and adequately deep, which the grass in the foreground is in fact bordering. The beast lived on Carr Hartley's game "farm" at Rumuruti and if not exactly tame, was at least broken to the presence of spectators. When I say that this is a white rhinoceros, I am reliant on hearsay; it was in fact a flat grey in hue. It would appear to be feeding, though I can't really see what on. It could be just taking the weight off its neck. The best rhinos have tick-birds as sort of rear-gunners perched on their rumps; these birds have bright red bills and they eat ticks, see?

NAKURU

In March 1955 I was posted to Nakuru, to stand in for the District Education Officer there, Alex Phillips, who was going on eight months' leave. I had in my hands the administration of three districts in the Rift Valley Province: Nakuru, Naivasha and Thomson's Falls, which contained about 90 African primary (Years 1–4) and 6 intermediate schools (Years 5–8). Those primary school pupils who failed the entrance exam to an intermediate school either dropped out of school and went home, or stayed on to try again next year (and the following year and the year after that . . .) getting more literate every year. The day-to-day administration of all these schools – recruitment of teachers, payment of wages, supply of equipment – had been farmed out to the Missions and all I had to do was act as secretary to the three District Education Boards, keep account of Government money, and travel around on tours of inspection. I visited each school twice in the time I was in Nakuru, my duties including judging the competition for the best school vegetable garden. I stayed in the best hotels or with friends. Not until I went on to Kitui did I have to rough it in rest-houses on a camp bed.

I made some good friends during my stay, including my Assistant Education Officers, Luke Ochido and Robert Matano. Robert was elected to the Kenya Parliament in 1961 and for many years held various ministerial posts. My best friends, and one of the few families with whom I kept in touch later in life, were Isabel and Harold Edwards and their two children, Fiona and Richard. Harold was a chemical engineer and worked at nearby diatomite mines, while Isabel taught at Nakuru European Primary School. They took me on picnics on the low hills overlooking Lake Nakuru, an alkaline lake inhabited mostly by flamingos. In the two pictures here

are Fiona and Richard with the lake in the distance; and a group of us enjoying tea – I appear to be wearing cycle clips or something to keep the *dudus* (creeping things) from crawling up my trousers, while Isabel, wrapped up warm (we were well over 5000 feet up), seems to be handing out the food.

The school gardens competition was set up to show children how to grow the less common types of vegetable on their own shambas at home, to improve their families' diet. My duties as examiner included assessing the size and quality of the carrots, cabbages, etc., in the garden and asking the children, in my best Swahili, about vegetable cultivation. One school on the shores of Lake Naivasha, the lake on which the flying-boats of Imperial Airways used to land between the wars, was coping with flooding when I arrived, and the headmaster had to wade out into the lake, bend down, grope around, and then come up holding a carrot for my inspection.

While inspecting schools around Naivasha, I stayed two nights in the Brown Trout Hotel on the edge of the Aberdare Forest, then a Mau-Mau stronghold. I was the only guest in the hotel, and I was given a bed in the Bridal Suite, a double bed which had the contours of a hammock. Otherwise I often stayed at Kijabe overnight with the family of Wellesley Devitt, the head of the American Africa Inland Mission in the Rift Valley. As an army padre in WWII, he had acquired an MC in Burma, and as a Kikuyu speaker was now involved in trying to negotiate some kind of cease-fire with the Mau-Mau forces in the Aberdare Forest. It was his sixteen-year-old daughter, Helen, who persuaded me to lead an expedition for her and her young friends at Kijabe to climb Mount Kilimanjaro.

There now follow some pages about my time in Nakuru.

DICKIE'S BUNGALOW

We are now back in the realm of "places where I have parked my car". I lived in this bungalow in Nakuru for a month or so: the tin roof and the plastered walls stamp it as being pre-1939, houses built later being all of tiles and stone. On the verandah is a desk I bought at an auction for 17 shillings: I have taken the drawers out in order to replace their bottoms, which were the habitation of woodworm. I used to wear the canopy of the Land Rover like that to keep some of the road dust out of the front compartment. I shared this accommodation with a Mr. Bird, known universally as "Dickie"; in the evenings we would sit together in the sitting-room and he would drink beer. I recall that he ran an old Renault with the gear lever sticking out of the dashboard. Despite Mr. Bird's cheery presence, it was a pretty dreary place, and I was glad to get away from it to the brighter atmosphere of a bungalow in the grounds of the European Primary School, and which is pictured on the next page.

On the left of this picture you see the packing case in which I used to transport my valuables whenever I was posted to a new place. The lid is propped against the left end of the case. Eventually the case was moved onto the verandah of the bungalow which you see behind the case. The omnivorous hens belonging to the servants of the occupants of the bungalow next door (not visible in the picture, neither the hens nor the servants nor the bungalow) discovered the case and used to camp out in it. The only plant in the garden which the hens didn't eat was a cactus-like spiny growth which is visible just in front of the car. You have seen the car before. I never had an egg from the hens but when eventually I came to move, and started cleaning the case out, I instantly became host to some 8,000 chicken mites, very minute but very ticklish. The net curtain effect on the windows is produced by wire mesh, which is meant to puzzle housebreakers. The bungalow is in the grounds of the European Primary School, Nakuru. The trees are eucalyptus—gum to you.

GIRAFFE

This was intended to be a world-beating animal photograph. Here was this gigantic giraffe, only a few yards away, and me having crept up on him in my Land-Rover, hoping to get a picture which would take its due place among the great. The giraffe is the tallest post in the picture and can be further identified by having four knobs at the top, two sprouting out vertically (horns) and two at an angle (ears). The low bushes near him (or her—too far away to be sure) are in fact trees: as I say, he (she?) was a tall fellow (girl?). Behind and beyond him/her is Lake Nakuru and the Mau escarpment, and above these are the clouds which come up from Lake Nyanza in the rains. The land is farm land, and a trifle thick with weeds as far as I can judge. I don't know the names of the weeds, but they probably include Mexican Marigolds, whose perfume is such as, once one has smelt it, pervades one's less comfortable dreams for many years afterwards. I am not sure whether the barbed-wire fence is there to keep the giraffes in or out, but if I had legs that long, I don't think such items would bother me.

HILLSIDE WITH TREES

This is a fairly straightforward hillside with trees photograph. Two cows have their heads well down over on the right: the trees are what I call common or garden thorn trees, with the flat tops which give the African landscape its singular character - every hill should have thorn trees. Tucked away up the hill on the left is a cluster of tiny circular huts, though their apparent smallness is a result of their being some way away: they are in fact quite large huts, each capable of accommodating a family of ten souls or more. In the foreground is an impressive array of weeds, probably Mexican Marigolds, with, as I have hinted before, a most unpleasant and pungent stink. The scene is the White Highlands near Nakuru in the Rift Valley. It looks like rain, I think.

While I was teaching at Kagumo, I was invited by one of my students who lived locally to visit his home. The home, from which my erudite student had sprung, was a round hut with low earth walls and a high thatched conical roof, which inside was thick with soot-laden hanging cobwebs.

THOMSON'S FALLS

High up on a plateau below the western slopes of the Aberdares, a sluggish river crawls along a marshy channel, a haunt of hippopotamus and other aquatic fowl. Then it suddenly arrives at this precipice and falls in a most beautiful cascade into a pool some 240 feet below. The falls gave their name to the nearby township, Thomson's Falls, now renamed Nyahururu. In time I became Education Officer for the Thomson's Falls district and used to be secretary to the District Education Board under the chairmanship of the District Commissioner, Brigadier Pat Hughes, but when I took this photograph I was just passing through. Anyway, who cares about such mundane things as Education Boards when one can sit and look at a waterfall like this? I hope nobody ever turns it into a power station.

No collection of photographs, not even this one, would be complete without a study of the local girls. These four were walking along a road through the forest at Thomson's Falls, laughing and chattering as by universal custom, when I sprang out of the undergrowth and frightened them into posing for me. (Don't ask me what I was doing in the undergrowth.) One girl has dropped the woven sisal bag in which she will carry home the shopping; this normally hangs down her back and is suspended from a leather band which goes across her forehead. Hair is worn short; the kerchiefs are generally coloured and so are the dresses: shoes were at this time neither cheap nor comfortable, and hence were usually only worn with Sunday best. It strikes me that the girl on the far right is somewhat long in the tooth and may be mum or even granny. The sun is nearly overhead, as the shadows show; after a while I caught the girls' bashfulness and sloped off to have lunch (but not I hasten to add in the undergrowth).

Visiting a Primary School near Thomson's Falls, I found a P.E. Class in action, with an audience. On the fence on the left hang the shirts of the boys in the class: sheltering among these are some of the village children who do not go to school, while beyond them is either a village adult who does not go to school, or else a student teacher finding out by observation how it should be done. I have a feeling that the cutie on the right may be part of the teacher's family; the other children are wearing nothing more than a length of khaki cloth ("amerikani" - forty years earlier it would have been a goat skin) knotted over one shoulder, a style that leaves the slit skirt absolutely nowhere. The little girl with her hands behind her head is holding the straps of the bag which she is carrying on her back; you may see the strap passing over the top of her head. Shopping training begins here at a young age. The object on the ground in front of the guy in the white shirt is probably a stick of low-grade sugar cane or some allied plant. The fence posts are most likely cedar, which are practically white-ant-proof. Haven't we seen that Land Rover before?

Those of you who skipped the previous page had better turn back if you want details of the little folk in this picture. I was supposed to be studying the teacher's technique in teaching P.E. (see next page), not taking photographs anyway. My visit to such a school as this was quite an event in the school calendar; the Bwana Elimu only put in an appearance about once a year if that: all visits were recorded in the logbook and the previous infrequency of visits was obvious. The general supervision of the school was in the capable hands of the Africa Inland Mission supervisors; this school would be overseen by Wells Devitt or Ed de Young from Kijabe. My main job here was to judge the annual school garden competition, which I did by prodding beetroots, inspecting carrots, and questioning a selection of the older children as to the value of encouraging such things as humus in the soil. "Where," you may ask, "is the guy in the white shirt?" Don't worry, he will be back. (See next page.)

One of the strongest impressions I had of the average African teacher, such as the one in this picture, was his loyalty and devotion to the children in his care, his steadfastness and his perseverance in the face of difficulty. Remember too that at this time in Kikuyu country his life was in constant danger: as a government servant the teacher was a sure target for the sharp-edged pangas of the Mau-Mau, and so too were his wife and children. His equipment was often primitive and inadequate and old; his chair might have a broken seat (or perhaps this was a special one they offered visitors such as me). His wee daughter has a duplicate in this picture, which was taken in fact before those on the two preceding pages, in which number two child has retreated to seek sanctuary with big sister on the approach of the weird-looking pale-pink-skinned creature from another world (me again). The boy nearest the camera is probably about the fifth incumbent of those shorts, which may see him through secondary school before they are handed down once more. I wonder if skirts have gone mini here yet? I hope so. Didn't I tell you white shirt would be back?

KWA DEVITT

This is the Devitts' house at Kijabe. Rev. Wellesley Devitt was Supervisor for the Africa Inland Mission schools in our part of the Rift Valley Province while I was stationed at Nakuru, and he lived in this house on the scarp face of the Rift Valley with his wife Edith and his daughter Helen, who at the age of fourteen was extremely beautiful and who confided in me her ambition to be an airline pilot. On occasions I was given a bed for the night here while I was on safari in the area, my room being behind the little window up there by the chimney. I have no idea of the purpose of the bits sticking out of the chimney; all I know is that they have nothing at all to do with closed-circuit television or with telling the time by the sun. Lunch was always on the stroke of noon and was primarily ice-cream and steak and kidney (I think) pie, although not always in that order. The girl on the right (seen here three-quarter body) is carrying a debe, still in its pre-roofing-tile shape. My guess is that the house, like most of the mission, was built by Wells Devitt with his own hands. (Note: "kwa" is the Swahili for "chez".)

RIFT VALLEY

When exiles from Kenya casually state that the country is the loveliest on earth, this is the kind of view which prompts them to make so confident an assertion. This is the view from the window of the little guest room in the Devitts' house in Kijabe mission, with the sun shining on the Rift Valley in the early morning. Beyond the trees of the mission grounds the land drops sharply away down the escarpment, a land of rough scrub abounding in Sodom apples and stunted broad-leaved trees. Then comes the floor of the Rift Valley, with a patch of cultivation on the right of the picture, but otherwise the domain of the Masai, who graze their herds upon it, among antelope of all kinds and attendant predators. In the middle ground is Mount Margaret, while towards the horizon rises the shape of Suswa, an extinct volcano of the same lineage as Kilimanjaro and Kenya, but of lesser stature. Only the faint blue bars of cloud presage the storms which may possibly break on the hills later in the day.

But the Rift Valley was not just a plain peppered with extinct volcanoes. To the north-west it rose towards the White Highlands at Londiani, the limit of my territory, and the subject of the painting on the cover of this book. (The white flowers in that picture are pyrethrum.)

KITUI

In January 1956 I was posted from Nakuru where I had been standing in for Alex Philips, now returned from leave, and sent to Kitui as District Education Officer there, replacing James Mbotela, who had returned to teaching. I was responsible for administering about 20 District Education Board schools, and for inspecting about the same number run either by the Africa Inland Mission or by the Catholic missionaries. I stayed in Kitui until March 1957 when I went on leave. I had one assistant E. O., a local man called Philip Syindu, an ex-headmaster, who looked after the southern half of the district.

The headmaster of Matinyani School, one of the six Intermediate Schools in the district, was Eliud Ngala Mwendwa, who had political ambitions and who, just after I left the district, was elected as a member of the Legislative Council or Parliament. He was one of the Ministers in the fifteen-man Cabinet that Kenya's first President Jomo Kenyatta formed after Kenya's independence in 1963. Except for Kenyatta's family, no other family has produced more Members of Parliament in Kenya than that of Ngala's father, ex-Senior Chief Mwendwa of Kitui, who sired more than 40 children with his twelve wives, and pretty well populated the whole village of Matinyani. As Minister for Labour in Kenyatta's government, Ngala Mwendwa is remembered best for setting up the Kenya Industrial Court that adjudicates on disputes between workers and employers.

Kitui District was African land, with no European settlement. The people were the Akamba, who were the only tribe never to have killed a European. The district lacked certain amenities. There was no electricity supply, no telephone contact, no metalled roads within 70 miles. The nearest railway was sixty miles away. Water was piped into Kitui township, but we lit the evenings with Tilley lamps and cooked on wood stoves, and I powered my electric gramophone turntable with a 12-volt car battery. We had radio contact with Nairobi, and an Italian, Luigi Bianchi, ran a motor repair business. In periods of heavy rain rivers flooded and we were cut off from neighbouring districts for several days at a time, since there were no bridges but only "drifts", concreted road-beds where a main road crossed a river.. However there was a good postal service and a fairly good bus service. An average altitude of 4000 ft meant that the weather was warm but not humid, the best climate in Kenya.

I inherited James Mbotela's bungalow which I shared with two other officers, one being Jimmy Dobbs, an policeman from Ireland. His speciality was performing "Phil the one-armed Fluter" at parties. The social centre of the European *boma* was the club, and on Saturday evenings a small group of us would put on humorous turns and sketches, written by ourselves. One member of the group was Hilda Meadows, district organiser of the women's club *Maendeleo ya Wanawake* (Women's Progress); another was my great friend John Byrne, District Officer, who died aged 40 of a brain tumour shortly after I left Kenya for good.

I spent most nights working in my office by the light of my Tilley lamp. As I approached the office block , I would be challenged by the *askari* on guard, and would reply "Bwana Elimu" – "Boss of Education". At nine o'clock every night a bugler would sound "Last Post", which I found a very moving experience.

One day on my travels I was presented with a cockerel which was an officially acceptable gift – there were strict rules on government officers accepting favours. Two nights later I was woken up in the middle of the night by a crowing cockerel, so I invited friends round for a chicken dinner on Saturday night. Early on Sunday morning I was woken up by a crowing cockerel. It turned out that the culprit belonged to my cook, Nzau, who was instructed to remove it or see it served up in its turn, sharing the fate of my own poor innocent bird, for a Saturday night meal.

DISTRICT EDUCATION OFFICES, KITUI.

This, despite all appearances, is not a ghost picture showing the spectre of the District Education Offices, Kitui. This is a simple, normal, double exposure. The prominent image is the above-mentioned D.E.O., Kitui. They occupied much of one side of a three-sided quadrangle (mathematicians are not allowed to comment on this) and were cool, and shaded from the glare of the overhead sun at midday by the verandah with its white pillars. In the centre of the quadrangle were rose bushes, although I forget whether or not they ever bore recognisable roses. The only roses I remember seeing in flower in Kenya were at the Mawingo Hotel in Nanyuki. Behind the office is a towering bush of bougainvillaea with deep red flowers from which a rose-coloured light was reflected through the windows, suffusing the interior of the office with a magical roseate glow. (I've been trying to work that sentence in somewhere for years, but somehow it doesn't read quite right. I'll have to try again sometime. Fewer roses, perhaps.) The office was a beautiful place to work in, anyhow. I had a most interesting staff working for me and together we churned out masses of paperwork in the course of the fifteen months I was there. My chief clerk's name was Julius and I managed to acquire some three or four underlings for him to order about, which he did with exemplary panache and efficiency. One of these underlings was an office boy, Kabau, a most pleasant young lad who unknown to us had a spare key to the cash box and lifted quite a lot of cash from it which he hid in the roof of his house until we found out about him and his key and got the police to get the cash back.

THE VILLAGE STREET

The village street in Kitui caught motionless in the light of the afternoon sun. The long shadows of the trees whose names I either never learnt or else never could remember stretch themselves across the roadway easily, slowly, like great cats settling down to rest in the heat of the torrid day. The ridges of the roadway are thrown into visibility by the angle of the sun, showing the different levels left by the cutting blade of the grader which smoothes over the rutted, pot-holed surface just before the projected coming of the rains. In the distance the shops owned by the Africans and the Somalis line the roadway, each with its verandah and open space in which the fruits of the neighbourhood and its other crops and its meat and its beer are displayed and bought and sold. The long open stretch of road separates these simpler buildings from the modern stores with plate-glass windows and cash registers owned by the Asian traders and manned by their extended and extensive families. In the cooler evenings the trees harbour a few singing birds who presumably are sensible enough in the hotter part of the day to save their breath for such more productive activities as panting and breathing. At least I do not have much of an impression of bird-song in Africa, but that could be, as usual, just my rotten memory.

In my usual incompetent manner I took this picture of the Kitui bus at the wrong time, when it was not only empty but stationary as well. In fact it looks as if it's undergoing engine inspection if not repairs. I should have photographed it when it was rattling by full of passengers, with its roof piled high with suit-cases and wooden bedsteads and crates full of chickens, all reached via the ladder at the back. I don't remember that anyone travelled on its roof, as they would have done in India perhaps, but its internal capacity was fairly elastic, and the driver was usually quite happy to cram in another passenger. The chassis must have been incredibly strong to survive the pot-holes at speed. The windows have blinds which could be rolled down to keep out at least some of the dust of travel. I myself never travelled on a bus of this type– when I did once need to travel I did so in the passenger seat of a lorry, with behind me a load of some thirty bodies standing or sitting in various stages of discomfort. An African friend who had been to London told me that two things had struck him about England – women did not carry their babies on their backs and people did not travel on the backs of lorries. He didn't mention the fact that you don't see many buses like this in London either.

Just as Osman Allu's shop in Nyeri provided the township with all it needed in the way of worldly goods, so in Kitui did the shop shown here whose owner's name escapes me – let us call him Yusuf Ali for want of anything better. Like most shops in Kenya it was run by an Indian trader, the aforementioned Y. Ali, who employed his own family as assistants, and who prided himself in being able to provide anything (i.e. anything). The comments I made earlier about Osman Allu apply equally to this store, which is the one which supplied me with French mustard. It too stocked anything from safety pins to tyres, and from walking sticks to wine. Fresh fruit, milk and meat were fetched from the local market if necessary. The only thing I ever had to take back was a bottle of Burgundy which I believe had been sitting in the window in the warm sunshine for several weeks and which had suffered accordingly.

Petrol was on sale just round the corner, supplied by pumps which were operated by hand, a long lever pulled to the left and to the right, about five pumps to the pint. (The township had no electricity.)

The name on the sign is Jackson Road, though who Jackson was I have no idea – he may well have been a former District Commissioner. The folk gathered behind the sign are probably past customers or potential customers, or locals waiting for their friends to pass by, bringing the chance of a chat, or maybe they are just out-of-towners waiting patiently for the bus (see previous page).

This is the school for children of Muslim parents living in and around Kitui township. Most of the parents would be Somali or coast Arab, nearly all engaged in the wholesale trade, running crops and other goods from across the Somaliland border and elsewhere. In fact I was told that my old Land Rover, which I sold locally when I went on home leave in 1957, was subsequently put to good use in carrying green gram around the district. I had no official interest in the school, it being run independently by a group of parents and worthy locals, who were answerable perhaps to the Provincial Education Officer, but certainly not to anyone as lowly as me. However, I must have been on good terms with the teachers since they agreed to allow me to peep inside the school and to pose for me with the children, who all look, as would be expected, delightfully intelligent and spotlessly clean.

DISTRICT COMMISSIONER

Here we see the wheels of government revolving. By far the biggest cog in the district was the District Commissioner, and here is Colonel John Balfour, District Commissioner of Kitui, right in the middle of the picture. Surrounding him are members of the local and tribal police forces, together with a selection of elders of the location in which the wheels are revolving on this particular day. Much of the discussion would centre on cattle, of which there were generally too many, and on roads, of which there were too few, and on schools, which was the reason why I was privileged to travel with the D. C. on this particular safari. In fact the cogent reason was that by travelling with the administrative circus I was able to save on my own travelling expenses, and this was greatly to be encouraged, the country being as poor as it was, which accounts for the roads being so few and likewise the schools, and for the cattle being so skinny and in need of being reduced in number so that those remaining got a decent share of the available grass. Col. Balfour looks as if he is waving a little flag, but I think appearances are deceptive here. Below his elbow can be seen someone else's hat, removed in honour of the D. C.'s presence, and in the background there is a line of whitewashed stones, intended to smarten the place up a bit. The fuzzy effect is largely caused by fossilised dust coating the photo negative. I got on well with Col. J. B. who used to share my taste in wine, squash, music and poetry. (Probably in women too, but I don't remember discussing these with him.)

For the benefit of those who can't focus this one properly, I state that this is myself standing with one foot on the neck (figuratively speaking, of course) of a baobab tree. I think I had some intention of recording for the benefit of non-travellers the immense size of the trunk of the tree, although there was always the danger that they might think that I was just thin. To prevent this from happening, I was very careful to bring my Land Rover into the picture as well. Come to think of it, I couldn't of course have taken this picture myself. It must have been my mpishi, Nzau, who took it. The Land Rover has an extra petrol can strapped on to the front nearside wing, filling stations being a rarity to the number of two in twelve thousand square miles. The tree is as big as it looks, though not very tall. There is a picture of a whole tree on another page.

"The baobab, the upside-down tree, standing pensive on the plain, wondering will it ever be the right way up again?"

Legend has it that the tree is actually growing upside down with its roots in the air, but an inspection of the bark doesn't really help to confirm the legend or show it to be false. How do you tell if a tree is growing upside down, anyway? I suppose if you dug down and found leaves sprouting at a depth of ten feet or so, you might be able to make out a case, but why tamper with a good legend?

I seem to recall that this was the site, already laid out and with the buildings erected, for a new school which a village wanted and which probably wouldn't be approved because there were no teachers available and a long waiting list against the time when they would be available. The bush has been cleared however and maybe the buildings would become a community centre meanwhile. There is my old Land Rover on the left recognisable by the EAK sign on the back flap, and my cook in the white shirt is standing in the middle ground, and on the right various village elders are standing around hopefully, proud of their new school and wondering where they might conjure up a teacher. I seem to recall again that hoping to further their hopes they hopefully made me a present of a sheep which I then illegally carried home and ate, sharing it with my friends. I think I christened the sheep Wilberforce. Or Samuel. The tree on the left is a baobab, mentioned on another page. See what I mean about the roots in the air? I don't know anything at all about the other trees, except that they look more normal, and have very small leaves, and that no one is likely to mistake the place for somewhere in Epping Forest.

MYSELF WITH TEACHERS

This is the obligatory picture of the author (right) in the company of prominent citizens of the locality (left and centre) on the occasion of the opening of a new school (background). The new headmaster, Geoffrey, is on the left and in the centre is his untrained (anonymous) assistant. Between them they would be responsible for the early education of a few dozen children from nearby, that is, within a radius of some dozen or twenty miles. I seem to remember that I had brought the untrained teacher from another school as a passenger in the back of my Land-Rover. My cook, Nzau, was always inviting people quite unknown to me to ride in my gari on my safaris: I acted I suppose as an unscheduled but highly welcome bus. I wonder how much the fare was. Anyway I assumed on this occasion that the aforesaid teacher was going on holiday or was off perhaps to see an aunt, whereas really he was being posted with my full approval to a new school, a fact I understood only after we had arrived. I suppose looking back that he could probably have claimed travelling expenses. I do not know what he is carrying in his hand, but it could be the bulk of his worldly goods. The building looks very attractive with its new thatch and the local equivalent of diamond-leaded panes. I do not look as attractive as I might have hoped. I won't say that I gave up wearing shorts as a result of seeing this photograph but I refrained thereafter from entering competitions for the sexiest knees. I do have feet. They just got excluded accidentally from the picture by my cameraman Nzau.

I have long forgotten, if I ever knew, why the children in this picture were raising their hands. Tentative conjectures include:

Hands up those who have seen this guy (me) before.

The sun rises/sets in that direction.

That is the roof of our school.

Hands up those who are here today.

There will be a prize for the pupil with the longest arm.

Hold up your toothbrushes.

And: If you feel like it, wave at the camera.

On the left is an open-plan classroom, with a desk obscurely visible in the shadow. Notice how the shadows are very short, indicating, as Sherlock Holmes would say, an overhead sun, my dear W., a symptom of mid-day.

The lighter-coloured patches to the left of the brick pillar are probably two little bags hanging on nails and containing somebody's lunch, and part of the teacher. The hill in the background is covered in scrub and a haze which is due to the sun creeping in at the lens of the camera. The school is covered in corrugated iron sheets attached to thin poles which serve as roof timbers. The children are covered in a velvety dark-brown skin, scarred here and there with thorn scratches and the attacks of biting insects, and dusty in the dry season with the red soil of the district, but warm to the view and putting to shame the pale washiness of the European's apology for skin. They are pleasant children, with the fire burning in their souls like all children who ever were wherever.

BUDDING STATESMAN

I guess it behoves me to be a bit more humble. Originally on the next page I had called this a forgotten part of Africa, but that would only mean I had forgotten where I had taken the photograph. This picture brought me up with a jerk, because it shows children starting out on the long journey which may conceivably by now have brought one or more of them into the conference rooms of the statesmen of the

world. Many of Kenya's twentieth century statesmen, politicians, and academics, began their education making the shapes of letters in the sand with their forefingers, and this picture also emphasises the handicaps of poverty which they had to overcome. I have a faint memory that the little one on the left may have been too young to be in school and was brought along by his big sister whose job it was to look after him. On the other hand no parent is going to lay out good money on school clothing, however skimpy, unless a child is officially enrolled as a pupil. It seems in fact more probable that he is either deep in thought or has already finished the writing exercise and being proud of the fact is giving his well-known imitation of a camel, who alone knoweth the hundredth name of God.

TWEEZERS

This one is slightly off centre but contains just enough of interest to make it worth including. Moving from back to front we have several items of note. A hillside covered in whatever passes for vegetation in this somewhat desolate, if not forgotten, part of Africa. A fence made with sticks fastened together with plaited strips of bark. A schoolroom set in its own garden, the latter consisting probably of no more than a little island of the afore-mentioned vegetation. Whatever it is it looks as if it needs cutting. The old boy (mzee) is not engaging in an indigenous form of Yoga but is plucking his beard with a pair of tweezers built of iron, on the same lines as some of those I'm sure I've seen in the Egyptian Room at the British Museum. He looks old enough to have been a boy before the British arrived in Kenya in around 1900, bringing with them schoolrooms and other trappings of Western education. The strip of tartan-style cloth which is wrapped round his loins is the common nether garment for men in these parts and is called a kikoi. Note that as a mark of his dignity as an mzee he is wearing sandals, though not, as many sandals were, made from an old car tyre. The children are kept bald for comfort and cleanliness in this climate. As for telling which are boys and which are girls (not always easy for me as a European), the boys wear shorts and the girls wear dresses. I cannot identify the object in the right foreground but I don't think I should be keen on going anywhere near it in bare feet.

REST HOUSE

This splendid rest house with its whitewashed walls and its tarred skirting where the rain might undermine the mud walls, and with its bordering stones painted white, had the honour of being slept in on this occasion not only by me but also by our illustrious District Commissioner, John Hickson-Mahony (who succeeded Col. John Balfour in this post) and by his assistant, John Byrne of beloved and happy memory, who died within two years. I know that this was the occasion because of the presence of two askaris on the verandah, these being the two nigh-invisible soldier gentlemen in the centre and not the two cooking pots (sufurias) on the ledge on the right. The minor piece of architecture at the back is the kitchen. The odd-looking patches in the sky and elsewhere are not freak clouds or false suns but patches of fungus which seem to have attacked the print in recent years. Notice on the ridge of the house a line of tin rectangles, these being fashioned (and flattened) from the all-purpose African debe or paraffin can. I'm sorry that J. H.-M., J. B and the others aren't in this picture. They were no doubt meting out law and order somewhere close by, while I had already inspected the local school and had a chat with the headmaster and had come back for an early evening beer, or more likely a Canada Dry Orange which I seem to remember was all the rage about this time. The bars on the windows are to stop lion getting in, not me getting out.

THE ROCK

One of the most fascinating features of Kitui District is the scattering of great primæval rocks which jut at intervals out of the landscape, with all the appearance of gigantic volcanic extrusions which remain untouched after the softer nondescript stuff they once extruded through has been worn away. In fact, this is what they generally are. Mind you, looking at them from a safe distance is one thing: sleeping right close to the base of one, wondering if there is going to be a midnight fall of boulders, is something quite different. Anyway this one as it happened held OK and we got away the following morning without casualties. I consider this to be a magnificent cliff, and not a bad photograph of it either. The lines across it are genuine and are not just scars created by a dirty lens. These suggest that the rock may not be extruded but folded, but folded or not it looks pretty firmly extruded to me. Its face doesn't invite you to climb it, unless you happen to be a spider or a limpet or Chris Bonnington, although you don't get much snow and ice at this altitude so that wouldn't be a problem. The thatched building at the back is a resthouse (q.v.) while that in the left foreground is a kitchen. The two Land Rovers parked outside the resthouse suggest that I had company that night, since I am certain I wasn't driving two cars. I wonder who the other car belonged to, where this place was, and whether it's still there. The rock looks fairly permanent: the houses tend to fall apart after about ten years, usually after a severe attack of the white ants. Very nasty.

ON AND OFF THE ROAD

When I said in the introduction that this would be a collection of "awful and uninteresting" pictures, I was not scratching for compliments. These three pictures bear out my claim.

On the left is a picture of the picturesque country to the west of Kitui township, in the Yatta location. It looks uninhabited but every night could be heard coming from it the sound of drumming, indicating the holding of village revels. The visual effect is somewhat marred by the intrusion of someone's elbow. I don't think it's mine since I was somewhere to the right of it, and it's not the right colour for Nzau's elbow. It must remain just a mystery elbow.

On the right is more scenery, probably in the Katse location, showing the mountainous nature of that area, and the lush vegetation which adorned the higher ground. Once again something has intruded. It doesn't look like a part of the landscape nor does it resemble an elbow: it could be a finger and thumb, but it is really anybody's guess. The faint smudge in the top left corner could be a vulture, in which case this possibly started out as being a bird picture.

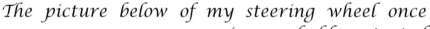

The picture below of my steering wheel once again probably started out as a picture of  something else, a captivating piece of African scenery, now faintly visible in the middle ground as a conical hill or two. Whatever it was it clearly warranted my stopping at the time and taking a snapshot at it through the windscreen. Anyway, it is a reasonably clear picture of my steering wheel and you can also see a chunk of dashboard below it. The white patch could be a butterfly or a discarded sweet paper or a bird dropping or the tip of a puddle in the roadside ditch. The flat-top bush could have been nibbled down to that shape or else it could be a Flat-top Bush.

TSEIKURU SCHOOL

The large building in the distance is a school, typical of those built in the early 1950's in Kitui District, made of brick and with a corrugated iron roof, and consisting of three classrooms, two teachers, and a store-room-cum-office. At the end of the building are two water tanks which catch rainwater from the roof, and these were, or should have been, an important source of drinking water for the whole local area. Unfortunately many of these schools and watertanks were built on very unstable so-called "black cotton" soil, and in the rainy season the soil moved and the floors and the walls of the schools and the tanks cracked. One headache was how to patch up the leaking tanks cheaply and effectively. A bigger headache at this school in Tseikuru however was the fact that the new and very dynamic chief had just conducted a recruiting campaign and had bumped up the numbers of children at the school from 16 in 1955 to 540 in 1956. With only two teachers in the school, this teacher/pupil ratio of 1/270 must have set some kind of record. However, bereft of its pupils, the school looks good. The school compound is in beautiful order, well fenced with dead and living wood: the road is lined with whitewashed stones. On the horizon are the hills of Embu, rising beyond the Tana valley. The white buildings to the right of the school are teachers' houses, and the thatched building is the previous school. I admit you don't see much evidence here of 540 children, but see next page.

As I mentioned on the previous page, a new and dynamic chief in Tseikuru had just conducted a recruiting campaign and had bumped up the numbers of children at the school from 16 in 1955 to 540 in 1956. In time most of these drifted away back home, but the results of the recruiting drive gave me an idea of how many children in the district never attended school. In fact the history of primary education in Kitui, if not in Kenya as a whole, was of very slow growth. The schools were there, the teachers were there, but pupils were very hard to recruit. Parents were unwilling to pay the reasonably small fee for their children to attend school, through an inability to see the point of education. The missions did their best to persuade their congregations to send their children to school, partly to ensure a supply of native-born pastors, much as the church in Europe did in the Middle Ages. Children who learned to read and write could after six or eight years in school possibly find work in the police and army or as clerks in local government offices, or even as teachers. A very few made their way through the system to university, but those who failed the entrance test for an Intermediate school after four years were turned loose to return to whatever work might be available, usually tending goats. When I suggested to a meeting of teachers that these children after four years of education were better fitted thereby for tending goats, it raised a laugh.

The urgent message which arrived from the headmaster at Tseikuru, asking how he was expected to teach 500-odd children with two teachers and three classrooms, sent me scurrying to view the situation for myself, inasmuch as an ageing Land Rover could be said to scurry over forty miles of rough track. The available staff were doing the best they could under the partial shade of a tree. While I was there a young mother brought along a three-year-old boy and asked the headmaster to take him in exchange for his seven-year-old sister, who was needed to look after the baby while the mother worked in her shamba (vegetable patch). The only help I had in all this from my superior officer was the advice not to accept fees until the pupil population had settled down, which it did eventually at around a fairly manageable 100 mark.

CHOO

And now for the prize of them all. Not just another "Where-my-Land-Rover-has-rusted" (sorry, rested, but on second thoughts, perhaps...) photograph in an interminable series, but a real piece of social comment. Here we are back again in Tseikuru with its 540 children in school, and with its chief anxious to put the place on the map. When I first visited the location, I slept in a spacious rest-house which was just about to succumb in its battle with the white ants and which had a neat line of scorpions moving about just beneath the sandy surface of the floor, and which looked out over the valley of the Tana River to the mountains of Meru District, all greens and blues and browns in the fierce glory and shimmering air of the African sunset. A scene of breath-taking beauty and one which I left with regret and returned to with heart-leaping anticipation.... Since my last visit the chief had improved the accommodation for government officers. In place of the crumbling old barn of a wooden rest house he had built a matchbox-sized new rest house in brick and concrete which I didn't sleep inside because, although I don't suffer from claustrophobia and so forth, I preferred to sleep on the verandah. And the view which was illuminated by the setting sun was no longer the fairy vista of valley and hill but a fine new long-drop lavatory building or "choo" planted bang in front of the resthouse to make it an easy journey in the wee small hours, I suppose. By the way, I looked at this shot many times before I saw the pensive guy who is walking out of the gate. Blind, I am.

A RIVER

Deep in the heart of the impenetrable African bush, where foot of white man has rarely if ever trod, flows a mighty river, full of cataracts and crocodile and hippopotamus and mosquitoes and mystic romance. Its beauty is legendary, its pools are fabulous, its passage lies through faery canyons below towering cliffs, and the poetic tongue falls mute at the sight of its Kubla Khan-esque waters. This shot does not perhaps show it to its full advantage, but it was cloudy at the time and I've mentioned before how capricious my camera becomes when pointed towards anything in less than 120% sunshine. It's a pity this view of the river isn't in colour because one could then contrast the dusty brown of the foliage of the trees lining its banks with the muddy brown of its waters, to say nothing of the slate-grey of the towering hill in the left background and the nondescript grey of the sky. That just about ties up the scene. Actually there is a faint discolouration in the sky which is very possibly Mount Kenya (see the road picture elsewhere). This is more of a puzzle picture than the road one. The road indisputably runs both ways. You are invited to guess which way the river is flowing, if flowing is the right word. I seem to remember that the water was definitely flowing or going in one direction and not just jiggling about. The lumpy things scattered about are rocks. On closer inspection I think I detect a bit of a cataract in the left foreground. Coo!

CATARACT

This shows the rest of the cataract whose vestigial toes were peeking out at the bottom left of the previous view. Again not doing much justice to the scene. These falls though were considered grand enough to warrant a signpost near Thika which said: "Grand Falls 56 miles". The signpost omitted to add that 55 of these miles lay along rough earth roads and that the last mile was negotiable only on foot, mainly owing to the fact that it was difficult to get roads to stay in situ for long on the run-in to the river (see next picture). The river was the Tana River and the falls were impressive on a minor scale, being the only lively water of any volume for miles around, although a little further upstream the river squeezed itself through a narrow ravine full of bubbling, boisterous water, before shooting over the edge of the falls, which is what you see it doing here, top left-hand corner. I liked it, anyway: it was more cosy than the Victoria Falls and more approachable than Niagara, neither of which I happen to have seen. This is one cataract I can claim to have been to, with no other sightseers around to spoil the pleasure that my cook and I gained from a silent and tranquil contemplation of this fine natural spectacle, a pleasure marred only by the fact that we'd left the beer back in the Land Rover. Actually I like this shot. At least the water looks animated, unlike a shot I've got of a Welsh falls at Conwy which looks frozen solid.

SOIL EROSION

Soil erosion! I hadn't seen soil erosion before, not on this scale. This patch of bare — and how bare! — earth lies about a quarter of a mile from the banks of the Tana River in Tharaka Location, in the northern part of Kitui district, and what you see here is the result of wind and rain battering on soil which is not really hospitable at the best of times and which tends to resist the attentions and attacks of stuff such as grass which just wants to put its roots down and find a permanent home. Only a few bushes have managed to ensnare a bushel or so of topsoil around their roots; the rest of the stuff is en route via the Tana River to the Indian Ocean two hundred miles downstream. (Who would be a bush? If soil erosion doesn't get you, the goats will.) The scale of this photograph is such that you could pick up the stone in the foreground and and hold it pretty comfortably in your fist. In the background top right is the sandy bed of a little stream, dry now but ready to carry water and mud off the surrounding land at a capital rate when the rains come. It is a replica in miniature of the many rivers of the district which flow only in the rainy season, and in whose dry beds in the long dry season the women dig wells from which they daily draw a gallon or two of murky water to service their family needs. Some women walk miles to the river, and then miles back home with a calabash of water on their heads. Attempts are being made to carry piped water to villages but this is a long and expensive process. Much of this piped water comes from sub-surface dams. A low dam is built across a river; the stretch above the dam fills with sand, and in the dry season the water trapped in this sand (see above, women with calabashes) is piped off.

DANCERS

No other scene I witnessed in Africa stands out in my memory as clearly as this one. By chance I was visiting a school in Mutha, a location in a remote corner of my district, hot and dry, and towards dusk I was told that a contest was to be held to choose a team of dancers to perform at the Red Cross fete to be held in the grounds of Government House, Nairobi. As a bureaucrat and therefore presumably impartial, I was invited to sit on the panel of judges. This picture shows the winning team in action, with a line of girls on the right, three drummers drumming, and behind the drummers on the left a line of boys. (The two nearest girls are mere infants, learning by doing.) In the centre, wearing a tartan-type kikoi, is the conductor. The girls wore no more than black skirts and various belts, necklaces, headbands and other ornaments made wampum-style from red and white beads. The rhythm was compelling, the movements were fierce, the dust rose in clouds from under the dancers' feet, and the audience were delighted, the women in the crowd showing their appreciation almost continuously with a shrill ululation, rarely heard except on such occasions. When my own bedtime arrived, I was told they would be dancing well on into the night. I retired to my camp bed regretfully, happy and privileged to have witnessed a popular entertainment which may have remained unchanged for centuries.

SAFARI - JANUARY 1956

It was pouring with rain as I loaded all my gear into the back of the Land Rover. With the help of my cook, Nzau, who was travelling with me, I finally packed in all the boxes, one containing food, another cooking and eating utensils, and another containing everything for which there was no room elsewhere - a canvas bath, a canvas wash-basin, a few books and a pillow. A bag with clothes and a sleeping-bag, a Primus stove, a Tilley pressure lamp and an assortment of folding frames for the camp-bed, bath, etc., filled up nooks and crannies. I put my briefcase bulging with files and a receipt book register on the centre seat of the car, Nzau settled down on the far seat, and I climbed into the driving seat, started the engine, put the car in gear and we moved away down the hill. The rain was still coming down at the rate of about an inch an hour. The canvas roof of the Land Rover leaked water over my feet as we drove out of Kitui.

Further down the road the rain slackened and the road surface became drier. There was less mud and eventually the mud gave way to dust. By the time we reached Matinyani, six miles out of Kitui, there was no more sign of rain and everything was dry.

We pulled off the road and drove up the path to the Intermediate School. This is a brick building with a concrete floor and a corrugated iron roof, built a few years ago but still not complete. Foundations have been dug for a new classroom and a staffroom, and I must find out soon how much money is available for building. The classroom is badly needed. At present three classrooms serve four classes and the lowest class meets in a banda, a building built on a frame of poles and indifferently thatched with grass. The white ants have climbed up the wall poles inside their little earth tunnels and are exploring the roof. When they have burrowed into the poles and eaten away the interior of each pole, leaving only a solid-looking shell, the banda will collapse.

[In the picture, Nzau, my cook, wearing an apron, is standing with a teacher beside my Land Rover. This is not my own old car but a new government Land Rover with an OHMS number plate, given for my use when my own car became too unreliable for journeys around the district.]

My business at the school was to select from those boys who had just joined Standard Five from the local primary schools, a half-dozen or so who would be sent to the Government Intermediate School in Kitui. This was the first intermediate school to be built in the District and it still has a European principal, and is for boys only. The boys who go there have the benefit of better teaching than is available in the other intermediate schools in the district, which number six. The boys I was after therefore had to be promising, of a good academic standard and young enough to qualify for secondary school when they had finished their four years in the intermediate school.

All the boys anxious to go to the Government school were lined up in front of me by Eliud Ngala Mwendwa, the African principal. I dismissed those who were obviously too old - those over thirteen would be over twenty when they sat for School Certificate - and from the remainder I selected seven who had gained reasonably good marks in the entrance examination. These seven were told to report as soon as possible to the principal of the

Government school, taking with them the sum of 145 shillings in fees. This sum would include the cost of boarding at the school for the year.

My next stop was at the Africa Inland Mission Intermediate School at Mitonguni. The Mission is an American body which is very active in these parts and has been established for some twenty-five years in the colony. Here the problem is more complicated. Not only do I have to choose entrants to the Government school but I also have to reduce to forty the numbers in a class which at present, owing to some misunderstanding, numbers fifty. I have to explain to some children that whereas my predecessor told them they had passed to go into Standard Five, they had in fact not done so and must leave school.

The children had not yet begun afternoon school when I arrived. I had left Kitui at about midday, and having now travelled about thirty miles, I was getting hungry. I sat in the staffroom of the school, a new brick building, and ate my chicken sandwiches, with which I was armed for just such an emergency. Nzau was foraging in the village for his own meal.

The task of sorting out Standard Five was less of a problem than I had feared. I was able to dispose of much of the surplus by sending half a dozen children to the Government school. One boy who was very young I sent back to his primary school, and another who seemed to have crept in on no authority at all I was forced to turn out. The selection process did not take very long.

A longer job was the sorting out of Standard IV in the adjacent primary school. A number of those who had returned to the class this year were coming back for a third attempt at the entrance examination to Standard V. Some of these were about fourteen or fifteen years old and stood no chance now of being admitted into Standard V, so I had to tell them there was no longer any room for them in school; that the primary school was for little children only; and that since they were no longer little children it was my painful duty to send them away. The Government does not guarantee schooling for Africans in Kenya: education is not yet compulsory, and only the select few pass into secondary school and take the School Certificate examination. Incidentally, quite a number of Europeans in Kenya do not know that African students sit for and pass this examination, often with distinction.

Ten miles along the road I pulled in at one of my own schools, run not by the missions but by the District Education Board of which I am the secretary and Executive Officer. The children were in the school shamba picking beans which were just about ripe. The recent rainfall has resulted in a big crop hereabouts and it seems that this year the usual famine, which hits the district at the end of the dry season and keeps many children at home without the energy to walk three or four miles to school and back every day, may not occur.

I stay long enough at the school to chat with the teachers and to find out their names, and then I hurry on to where I want to spend the night. The main object of this safari is to visit the schools in the Northern Division of the District, the furthest of which lies a hundred miles away from Kitui. Fifteen miles on I reach Muingi, a small market and trading centre which lies on the main road from Nairobi to Lamu on the coast. Here one may purchase petrol from the Indian traders who have shops, or "dukas", in the centre. I fill up with enough petrol to take me into the far north and back. My tank holds ten gallons and at a rate of twenty-one miles to the gallon allows me a range of two hundred and ten miles. There is no other petrol available from now until I return to Muingi, so I fill right up and press on.

The roads on which I had been travelling up to now are maintained by the Public Works Department. They are laid down with a surface of murram, which is crushed rock, and are kept reasonably smooth by the "graders", large machines with a bulldozer action which scrape off the surface wrinkles every so often and fill in the ruts and potholes. The road which I took now was a track maintained by the local chief, such maintenance taking the form of preventing the grass from growing too far into the centre of the track and of filling in the deeper ruts and holes. This work is done by hand and is partially effective. The chief characteristic of the road is the abundance of little channels worn by streamlets which flow across the road when it rains. These streamlets are not very large nor are the channels very deep, but a succession of these channels imparts a pitching motion to a Land Rover which is the reverse of comfortable. However I will call this one a road in contrast to the track which I met later on. A road does not have grass and little bushes growing in the centre between the wheel tracks. The track I encountered eventually does.

The scenery was growing more picturesque. From Kitui itself one sees little more than a plateau extending to the horizon. Twenty miles out one reaches the edge of the plateau and the country is more broken. In the gap between two hills I could see that beyond a valley there lay a high cliff and a high summit; as we went further along the road the whole of the escarpment came into view, deep in shadow in the late afternoon light. Most of the nearer hills, covered in scrub and rough grass, were crowned with massive slabs of bare, grey rock. The hills rose sharply from the plain and their sides were often nearly vertical. The country generally was otherwise rather flat or at best undulating and covered with low thorn bushes or stunted trees; flowers were rare and occurred in patches; long coarse grass provided grazing for sundry small herds of cows or sheep or goats, tended by small boys clothed in pieces of black cloth wrapped round their waists. These boys would stand and gaze at the car as it rattled by and would perhaps wave at us, sometimes grinning, sometimes with impassive faces. Here and there a group of huts showed its roofs above the bush lining the roadside, and a woman dressed in black or in a red-brown blanket, with a baby slung on her back inside a length of cloth, would climb off the road up onto the bank and into safety until we had passed.

A considerable number of cattle were being driven along the road in the direction of Muingi in preparation, as we learned later, for the cattle auction which was being held on the following day. It was the older men dressed in shirts above and blankets worn kiltwise below the waist who were driving these herds; at our approach they hustled the beasts off the road and waited for us to pass. I had the impression that we were disturbing the pattern of life which had satisfied these people for centuries past, and were treated as mere birds of passage, as indeed we are.

After twenty-four miles of pushing ahead we came to Waita which boasts a D.E.B. school. The school is a quarter of a mile off the main road on a rise and we drove up looking for the teacher. He was not in his house. A small boy directed us down to the village where I recognised the teacher in a small group by his general appearance of being better dressed and better groomed than the average. He seemed neither surprised nor overjoyed at seeing me but thawed out later. He suggested I slept in the rest house built and maintained by the local chief for the use of government officers travelling on safari. I asked whether I could buy any food in the village which appeared to include a few shops. The teacher said that I could not buy European food there although I learned the following day that he had plenty of beans growing in the school shamba which I could have bought from him. That night I ate baked beans and corned beef. The teacher did in fact bring me some milk from the cow which was kept near the

A school, possibly at Waita

49

school, and also a fly switch to scare away the flies which were enjoying the heat of the last rays of the sun which were just then striking on the door and the west wall of the building. The camp bed was set up, the lamp was lit, the Primus stove was lit, the camp table was fitted together. The tea was brewed, the milk was boiled, two boxes were drawn up to the table and I sat down to chat to the teacher, Henry Munyalo, over a cup of very welcome tea.

We discussed a number of things, beginning with personalities - how long he had been teaching (seventeen years), how long I had been in the colony (three years), which people in other places we both knew - and proceeding then to the useful part of the session from the point of view of both of us - the teacher's problems and the structure of the society in which he was required to do his work. I learned a lot about the home background of the children, the character of the local chief, and the state of repair of the school building. This last is a problem which apparently concerns me, since with money collected from the local people I am expected to employ a builder to do the necessary repairs.

Henry had brought me a chicken (live). I had earlier mentioned eggs in a hopeful tone of voice when I had asked about food for sale; the present of a chicken seemed to raise problems. It would hardly cook in time to be eaten tonight; on the other hand I did not look forward to carrying it as a passenger on the journey the following day, since a Land Rover is at the best of times, unless stationary, very unlike a peaceful chicken run. Nzau however took the fowl in hand and used a length of sisal to tie it to one of the poles which supported the roof. In this condition it spent the rest of the night.

The rest-house was a single room built of mud and wattle. Actually the wood used for the frame of the building cannot have been wattle, which does not grow in this part of Kenya; but the term is widely used to describe a common form of building construction. A frame is erected thus - poles are set in the ground at intervals and these support the roof. Smaller branches are either interwoven with these uprights in the manner in which hurdles are made; or more often are bound to the uprights on both sides to form a sort of double fence around the building. This double fence is packed inside with mud, which may be mixed with cow dung, and more mud is smeared on the inside and the outside to give a wall about one foot thick. The roof is usually of thatch or sometimes of corrugated iron, fastened on to the roof timbers. The ridge may be supported by poles set up in the centre of the floor of the building. This particular rest-house was thatched and had a sand floor; the walls were whitewashed on the inside and the outside, and the whole was reminiscent of the insect house at the zoo, a Whipsnade sort of zoo in which the animals are not confined but run wild. Certainly there is plenty of company in these rest-houses - flies, ants, termites, moths, beetles, spiders, mosquitoes, bugs, ticks, gnats, scorpions, and various other nameless creepies and crawlies, all conspiring to welcome you and make you feel at home, by flocking around and attracting your attention lest you should feel lonely. One gets used to them and ignores them and they eventually go away disappointed, and play their own little predatory games, which are very interesting to watch. I personally feel that these insects and the like are intriguing creatures, and I am quite willing to share my sleeping quarters with them as long as they keep their distance and do not drop into my tea or down my neck. I can spend minutes on end watching their antics and examining their markings, which on the moths are very beautiful, but after a while the interest slackens and I turn my attention away and on to more pressing subjects such as food.

When Henry had finally excused himself from the table and gone off home, I ate the corned beef and baked beans which Nzau had heated up, chewed a piece of chocolate, bathed thoroughly in about two inches of water, and settled down to read a book, "No Highway" by Neville Shute.

For some forty minutes I sat on my upturned box, made more comfortable to sit on by one of the seats from the Land Rover, and, leaning back on one of the central supporting posts, I had a quiet read. At about ten I put the book away, visited the local hole-in-the-ground, cleaned my teeth, put on my pyjamas (which I consider to be a justifiable luxury), and edged my way under the mosquito net on to the camp bed. My camp bed is rather old and it is necessary to put one's weight initially on the part which I reinforced for the purpose with lengths of webbing. Then comes the problem of getting into the sleeping bag, and finally of tucking in

On the banks of the Tana River

the net all round so that the risk of being woken up later by a buzzing in the ears or a tickling on the nose is reduced to a minimum. The lamp is put out, the net is pushed under the sleeping bag, the head is lowered on to the pillow, and the eyes are closed. From outside comes the constant chirping of a myriad grasshoppers, which has formed a half-unnoticed background to the evening's activities and which now springs on to one's consciousness as one lies awake in the little room with the moonlight streaming in through the holes in the wall which serve as windows and ventilators and ways in and out for various species of flying bugs. Occasionally the captive chicken on the far side of the room would flutter its wings and wake me from the sleep into which I was in danger of dropping; in short, everything conspired to prevent my obtaining that deep sleep which would send me out on the morrow fit and ready to deal with the many problems which would most surely face me: which road to take, what to advise for stubborn parents who insisted their sixteen-year-old sons stay in Standard IV for yet another year, what comment to make on half an acre of millet which seemed to be doing well enough without my comments. The most effective opposition came from the temperature: at around three in the morning I awoke soaked in perspiration and threw off as much of the sleeping bag as it is possible to throw off when a sleeping bag is tied fairly tightly around one's neck. At six in the morning I awoke with a pale light shining in through the windows and the door, which latter was now wide open and letting in a fair draught which was cooling my ribs and my toes in such a way as to make further sleep impossible. At seven I rose and lit the stove for tea. Nzau came in some minutes later and took the tea in hand while I climbed back into bed for those luxurious last five minutes which are worth so very much in psychological value.

I shaved, washed, dressed, drank my tea, and sat down to a breakfast of porridge and toast and marmalade, or rather bread and marmalade. Then I left Nzau to start the packing while I drove up to the school to catch the children arriving. I was too late for that and the children were in assembly when I arrived, lined up in front of the flagstaff, and preparing to march off to the classrooms. They were of various shapes and sizes, these children. Some had shaven heads, while the rest had tight short black curls, boys and girls the same. In fact I should have had difficulty in telling the boys from the girls, had it not been for the difference in dress. All the girls had managed to acquire cotton frocks, some from the local shops, others handed down from their older sisters, others from the capable hands of their dress-making mothers. Most of them wore gaily-coloured handkerchiefs on their heads. The boys wore more varied dress. Some, the few, had shirts and shorts. Torn shirts, dirty shirts, shorts with holes in, shorts with patches in, shorts with a greater area of patch than original, but still recognisably shorts. These were the elite. Others had shorts only, others had shirts only. One boy was wearing a shirt which must have belonged to a giant of a man. It was certainly a comprehensive garment. It just managed to hang on his shoulders and the neckline reached down to his navel. The sleeves were rolled up and the rolls hung heavily from his wrists like a Chinaman's sleeves. The front of his shirt just allowed his toes to peep out as he trotted along, and the tail of the shirt swept the ground behind him like an emperor's train. Had he been an inch shorter he would have tripped up at every step. The shirt appeared to be made from blue and white ticking: it may or may not have been washed since the day it was bought, but the wearer was justly proud of it. It was a symbol of wealth by day and a blanket by night, and a protection against the winds in the cool season. It could be discarded or donned without the effort of unbuttoning or fastening up. Above all it gave its wearer an air of dignity and sophistication which he himself could hardly have appreciated. And if in its seams it happened to shelter many wee creeping creatures, I have no doubt that the wearer did not begrudge them their residence, since in that mighty shirt there was room for all and to spare.

One boy did very well by disposing with the work of tailors and relying for his warmth and dignity on a length of black cloth which he kept or tried to keep wrapped round his tummy. His tummy protruded well out from the rest of his front and he had to be content with fastening the cloth around his hips. His waist was well up around his chest and was in no way the place to wrap a piece of cloth: wrapped around his hips the cloth covered his buttocks behind and satisfied the demands of decency before. Not that that worried him in the least: every five minutes he would stand up, remove the cloth, shake it, and replace it around his hips. Then he would get on with his work quite happily and unconcernedly. By contrast, all the girls were very modest and kept their dresses pulled well down over their knees. Those who had inherited the dresses from older, and taller, sisters, found no difficulty in doing this.

Nzau beside the Tana River cataract

I followed the children and the teacher into the school. For the older children the teacher had written some arithmetic problems on the blackboard and the children were already wiping their slates clean with a bit of spit and a handy corner of one of their garments, ready to begin scratching away with their slate pencils. The teacher by now was teaching the smaller children their numbers. These children had only been in school for a week (the school year starts in January) but already they were all able to count up to ten in their own language, Kikamba. The teacher held up a card with two elephants painted on it. "How many?" he asked the children. "Two," came back the answer. He then turned the card over and showed the class two large black dots on the reverse. "How many?" Again the right answer. Then he turned to the blackboard and drawing two dots wrote beneath them the figure "2". "What does this say?" and so with the other numbers up to ten. Finally the children counted from one to ten in chorus. "Imwe, ili, itatu, inya, itano, thandatu, mwonza, nyanya, kenda, ikumi".

The teacher was on his own today because his assistant was applying to be trained and had gone to Kitui for an interview with the principal of the Teacher Training Centre. This meant the teacher had to teach two classes simultaneously, and now went off to deal with the older children who had finished their arithmetic in the other classroom and were needing attention. The younger children were left to amuse themselves, which they did very well. One child came out in front of the class and began to tell in his own language a story, presumably a traditional legend which he had been taught at home. The story lasted a few minutes; then another child came forward and spoke, and so on until the teacher returned. I was surprised at the ease with which the children told these stories. Not only did they speak with remarkable fluency but they also put a wealth of expression into their voice during the telling. They appeared to be at that early age just good actors. And they enjoyed themselves thoroughly during the telling. The children listening were very well behaved and did not interrupt but gave the speaker a good hearing and a round of applause at the end.

Now the children went outside to consolidate their knowledge of number. Sitting on the ground, they each began to write their numbers in the sand with their fingers. The teacher had a blackboard which he propped up before the children and on which he wrote the numbers for the children to copy. Then he went round helping those children who were writing their numbers sideways or upside down or back to front while I interviewed an applicant for a job. A young fellow who had just finished intermediate school wanted a temporary post as a teacher, and so I promised to take him on trial to replace the teacher who was going for training.

I now had to complete my business at the school and be on my way to the next school. The teacher, Henry, left the children to play around outside and began to conduct me round the school grounds. First we went to the school shamba (garden) which was growing millet and maize and beans and sunflowers and castor oil seeds. Everything seemed to be growing well and I managed an intelligent comment on the millet. I made a few suggestions about the next planting and discussed plans for the better layout of the ground: then we left the shamba and visited the cattle boma. This was a small cattle shed with two cows and a manure stack nearby. The shed had not been cleaned for some time and I told the teacher to keep it clean and to remove the manure at least once a week. The manure will be dug into the shamba partly to increase the yield and partly to retain as much moisture in the soil as possible during the dry season.

I wrote my observations in the school log-book together with my suggestions and instructions to the teacher, shook hands with him, and drove back to the rest-house where I picked up my luggage and Nzau. Then we drove on to the road and continued our journey north.

[That's all I wrote about that journey. I was four more days driving round the district as far as Tseikuru and Tharaka in the far north and then back. Tharaka location is/was home to a small group of perhaps 4000 people who had their own language, distinct from those languages such as Kikamba and Kiembu spoken in neighbouring locations. The only book published at that time in Kitharaka was St. John's Gospel, translated by the first resident missionaries.]

However, I wrote some more about Kitui and its schools in general, in the following year, and on the following pages is what I wrote as an appendix to the account which appears above.

KITUI 1957

I think our District, Kitui, was the happiest in all Kenya. Certainly the people were always smiling, from old Petro Mangole, who was the local agent for the East African Breweries and who ran a prosperous beer-shop of his own, to the barefooted children playing in the entrance to the little round thatched hut in which they had been born. The women trudging along the dusty roads to market, carrying on their backs great baskets full of maize or millet, or huge bunches of bananas, with their babies slung straddle-legged across their stomachs, sang as they went, over much of the ten to fifteen-mile journey. The old men, listening to the District Commissioner in a baraza, would nod their heads as each point was made, and smile to each other, and sniff contentedly the snuff which they kept in little carved wooden bottles which hung on the end of a thong, or which was carried tucked neatly into a large hole in the lobe of their ear. And in the schools the children would smile at the white stranger who stood inside the door and who very diffidently greeted them in their own tongue which he was painfully acquiring. "N'ũvoo?" A moment of surprise; the smiles widened into grins, and the reply came in chorus: "Ĩĩ, nesa!" ("Is it good news?" "Yes, nicely!") "Ĩkalai nthi." (Sit down.) "Asanda, Vwana." (Thank you, sir.) And with a scuffling the children would sit down, three or four to a desk, with one eye on the stranger and a weather eye on the teacher.

For sixteen months, until I was due for home leave, I had the pleasure of being the white stranger, and of trying to help the schools to more efficient work and to a greater degree of usefulness in the District. Ours was a backward district compared to some of our neighbours; eighty-five schools to serve a population of a quarter of a million, only nine thousand children in school out of a possible eighty thousand. Thirty thousand pounds to spend in a year on salaries and equipment and incidental expenses; six thousand pounds to spend on development, on the building of new schools and on the maintenance and improvement of existing ones. Two hundred teachers of whom only sixty per cent had any training; and of these two hundred only twenty were women. An annual wastage of, say, a dozen teachers; and no more than twenty new teachers a year coming from training. These are the bare figures and in terms of these may be stated precisely the problem of education in Kenya.

It is easy when one is out of the hurly-burly of office work and safari to question the policy of the Education Department and the allocation of money to African and to European education in Kenya. I have no brief whatsoever to talk about policy; all I can do is accept, as I had to, the poverty of the African community, especially in Kitui, and to work as best I could within the confines of financial stringency to attain higher and even higher standards with whatever money we were given. And that this was possible was and is due solely to the professional pride and loyalty shown by the teaching staff in the District. Fortunately the teachers usually had the support of the chief and of the other leaders in the community, who realised the value of the work the teacher was doing, and could usually be persuaded to help the teacher in his work, and who indeed were enthusiastic about doing so once they had been shown where the need lay. And the enthusiasm for education was gradually coming to be shared both by children and by parents alike.

To understand the stage of growth in the school system when I arrived in Kitui in 1956, I found it necessary to turn back to the history books and to the annual reports of the District which had been published from 1906 onwards. As long ago as 1848 Krapf and his companions were welcomed on the hill where the District Offices now stand, and were beyond doubt the first Europeans to set foot in this part of Africa. From here they looked northward and saw the snow-capped peaks of Mount Kenya: from here, far to the south, they could see the great white dome of Kilimanjaro. Rhino, elephant and lion abounded; beyond the Athi River were the plains where the Masai tended their cattle, plains which in addition swarmed with hundreds of thousands of head of buck, zebra, buffalo, giraffe, and pig. And here in Kitui the migrant Akamba were beginning to settle, to sow their small crops of millet, and hunt small game with their bows and arrows, just as many still do today.

By the 1880's the Leipzig Lutheran Mission had built a church and a mission house in Ikutha, in the south of the district, and the church building was still being used as a school in 1956. The missionaries held church services and persuaded the children to come into school to learn to read the Bible and to write, and to learn a few simple crafts such as carpentering and sewing. The fortunes of the mission varied; they must have made converts, and no doubt the children came to learn to read and write and then wandered off again to tend the goats, to till the fields, and to hunt the light-footed gazelles with their little bows and little poisoned arrows. The missionaries also came and went; behind the mission house is a little plot fenced off, where the school children still cut the grass around the graves. Some of the graves are marked by the stumps of termite-eaten wood, the remains of wooden crosses. There are four tombstones on four graves, two long, two short. Two children are buried there, a brother and sister, both of whom died within a few months of their birth. Two men are buried beside them, victims of malaria and overwork. The women seem to have been stronger. But the work went on, from the closing years of the nineteenth century, as is proved by the dates on the gravestones, until the closing months of 1914, when the German missionaries were interned as aliens and the mission was closed down, to be restarted under the Americans in the following year.

In 1898 a government officer walked the seventy-odd miles from the neighbouring district of Machakos, which has always been our big brother, to open a District Office in Kitui. The office was built of mud on a wattle framework and had a thatched roof: the offices now are all built in cement and brick, plastered inside and out, with concrete floors and tiled roofs. The District Officer's house too was built of mud, but soon aspired to a tin roof, and from this humble beginning the administration of Kitui District developed.

In 1906 a Government school was opened with a native (sic) teacher; in those days the word "native" nearly always meant "African". Nowadays when so many people of the immigrant races claim Kenya as their birthplace, it is more accurate and more polite to speak of the Africans as such: the word "native" is dropping out of at least official use. The native teacher recruited his first pupils from the sons of chiefs: even today one of the chiefs has forty-two sons, so the field of recruitment must have been wide enough in those far-off days. The school jogged along; shortly after the end of the 1914-18 war, the teacher was taken away and the school closed for a year. It reopened in 1920 and grew slowly into a primary school which drew its recruits from the bush schools which were being run elsewhere in the district by the missions.

The children who attended these bush schools must have been very bewildered at what went on. Clutching a broken piece of slate in one hand and a tiny stub of slate pencil in the other, sitting naked or half-naked on the ground, gazing with awe at the semi-literate teacher who scratched letters on a tiny square of blackboard and who bade the children copy them; trudging back home over five or ten or more miles on Friday, and trudging back to school again on Monday, carrying a little bag of millet to last them as food for the week, these children nevertheless sometimes grew into scholars, graduated from the bush school to the Government Primary School, from there went to Machakos where there was an elementary school, and eventually went one of two ways. There was a chance for a very few to go to secondary school and thence to college or even to a university in Britain. Most however returned to Kitui, some as clerks in the district office, others as teachers to teach the next generation and to perpetuate the process which they themselves had endured. They brought back strange knowledge, exotic dress, a new language (English, to add to Kikamba and Swahili), tales of romance and adventure, the broad range of the white man's arts, which they settled down to pass on to the little naked children who crowded into the tiny thatched hut which was their classroom.

Up to this time all the bush schools were run by the missions, who established schools wherever they had a congregation. Some schools flourished, particularly those which were associated with the larger churches, but on the whole the local people could be persuaded only with difficulty to send their children to school. Some outlying schools died from lack of support and closed, and for nearly twenty years between the wars, there were no more than twenty schools open in Kitui District at any one time.

The decade from 1940 onwards saw a great change in Kitui. I am not sure why this should be so: I think many factors were working about this time. At any rate a growth could be seen in the interest in schools taken by parents, some of whom had served with the armed forces, and also by Government officers, and more money for education was found in the post-war years. Pressure by the missions on the Education Department of the colony resulted in more young men being admitted to the teacher training centres, and as more teachers came from training, new schools could be opened. The annual output of teachers from Kitui rose from two or three before 1948 to ten or twelve in 1949 and onwards. This was also the time of the Beecher report, published in 1949, which laid down the lines for development over the following ten years and gave guidance to a new and energetic District Commissioner for Kitui who set about extending the network of schools to the furthest corners of the district. And finally a European officer had been posted to take over the government school and to supervise the running of the non-mission schools which were beginning to grow up, especially in the remoter locations.

For purposes of administration Kitui district was divided into twenty-three locations, each with its chief appointed by the district commissioner. The locations were grouped into four divisions, each under a district officer. By 1953 each location had its own school, and it was possible to say that no child lived more than twenty or thirty miles from a school: and that this permitted any child in the district to go to school is shown by the fact that even today (1956) children may walk twenty miles or more to school at the beginning and end of each week. In 1949 the Northern Division, comprising six locations, had three schools; by 1953 there were seven. The Eastern Division had only one school in 1949; by 1953 there were five. The Central and Southern Divisions were well supplied with schools since the American mission was strong in these divisions.

When a new school is to be opened in this part of Africa, the procedure is simple. The school manager goes with the chief to view the site chosen for the school. An approximate siting has already been made by the District Education Board, who decide which location needs a new school: an application by the chief is probably already in the hands of the Education Officer. The chief knows where the need for a school is greatest; there are few towns in the district and most of the people live in clusters of huts which are usually hidden from the road. As a result of this you may believe you are driving through uninhabited country whereas in fact there are dozens of huts on either side of the road, all hidden by the intervening bush. So when one goes to select a site for a school, one accepts the word of the chief that there is an adequate supply of children close at hand, that is, within a distance of a few miles, to provide a new class every year.

In a flat space in the middle of this seemingly deserted countryside, I as Education Officer would agree the siting of the school. The building was to have two rooms, each twenty-five feet by twenty, with a store and office between them ten feet wide: this gave a building sixty feet long by twenty feet broad. The sun should pass over the length of the building so it was set east and west: the doors would be on the side nearest the road. An old man would drive in pegs to mark the corners: I would pace out the distances; then a gang of men armed with pangas, the broad long knives which have so many uses in Kenya, from digging holes to foul murder, would squat down on their heels and begin to dig holes for the poles along the line of the walls. Others would go and cut the poles, slender trees, six inches in diameter and twelve feet long: the bark was stripped from them, they were set on end in the holes, and the holes filled in with earth, pressed down to hold the poles firmly in position. While digging or chopping the men would sing - a lilting solo, repeated in chorus, a question, a response, a long statement punctuated by shouts of agreement or joy. The work went on: once the poles were set up the wall-plate would go on, secured with strips of bark, or with six-inch nails if the funds ran to them. Then long supple branches were lashed to the sides of the poles, inside and out, lashed horizontally with bark strips at intervals of six or nine inches, with spaces left for windows and doors. Next, on would go the roof timbers, the ridge perhaps supported with stout poles in the middle of the classroom, the beams and ledgers secured with nails, and then long branches lashed across with bark. Then the thatchers would get busy: loads of grass were cut and carried from the hillsides and river banks by the women, each woman bent double under a huge bale of grass; and with this grass the thatchers put on a neat covering a foot thick, capable of turning the heaviest rain, which in these parts, if it does rain at all, may often fall for hours at the rate of an inch an hour. And finally the plasterers, using earth dug nearby and water carried from the river in gourds and bottles by the women, would mix their mud and use it to build up the walls. The space between the branches lashed to the poles would be filled in first; when the walls had risen to eight or nine feet, the inside and outside would be plastered carefully with mud to a smooth finish, with no trace of the framework visible, save at the level of the windows. Eventually the walls would be whitewashed, and then the children would bring water and stamp down the floor to a hard surface of mud, mixed perhaps with cow dung and ashes.

Next the teacher's house would be built in the same way: a two-roomed house with a kitchen hut nearby. Finally the latrines would be built - a deep and wide pit, with planks across the mouth and a hut built thereon.

A lorry would bring stationery and books, desks and chairs, blackboards, tables for the teachers, and two cupboards for equipment, much of the furniture being built in the carpenter's shop attached to the Education Office. And at last on the appointed day, the children would come, dressed sometimes in new clothes for the occasion, with chubby cheeks and gleaming teeth, heads shaved, feet bare, clutching in a rolled-up piece of cloth their school fees of a shilling or two. The teacher would enter their names in the register, collect the money, give each child a pencil and two exercise books, and school would begin.

The seventy-odd primary schools scattered over the district were of all shapes and sizes: most of them began in the way I have described, being built of mud and wattle with a thatched roof. There were quite a number which had been built years before in this way and which were still being used - the thatch leaked and the white ants were eating away the supports, but the children still came and sat in the draughty classrooms and seemed happy. On the other hand many of the District Education Board schools which had been built most recently had permanent buildings. Those which served the outer locations in the Northern and Eastern Divisions in particular had proper foundations, cement floors, brick or stone walls, sawn timber for beams and rafters and corrugated iron roofs. By the time I saw them, many were in bad need of repair and repainting, although the local people were proud of them. They had been built at the instigation of a former enthusiastic District Commissioner, but many were built on "black cotton soil" which was notoriously unstable in the rainy season. The raft of concrete on which the schools were built had often cracked and the walls too had cracked. (So also had the big round brick-built water tanks designed to take and store rain water from the roof. I was frequently asked if I could repair these, but I had no idea where the funding for repairs would come from.)

Each school required a school manager. He was responsible for building the school and equipping it and finding teachers. If the school was efficient, the manager could apply for grant-in-aid, which could be used to pay the teachers' salaries and buy books and other expendable and consumable equipment for the school. Many schools in Kenya are run by missions, and the manager of these schools is the head of the local mission. In the settled areas, a European farmer may build a school for the African children living on his farm and roundabouts, and he then is the manager of the school. Alternatively, a school may be managed by the District Education Board, which means that the District Education Officer, as executive officer of the Board, is in effect responsible for the running of a number of schools. District Education Board schools are usually found in places where mission influence is weak or in which missions are not working at all; or where the interests of two rival missions clash, in which case the school is managed by the D.E.B. as an impartial body.

As soon as I could tear myself away from the office, where a thousand things cried out for my attention, I set out in my little old Land Rover (and I use the adjectives literally and not from mere sentiment,) to tour, for choice, the Northern Division, where rumour had it a sudden enthusiasm for education was creating problems of accommodation. But more of this later.

The district is two hundred miles from north to south, and some seventy miles broad. In shape it is something like a lozenge but a lozenge some 12 000 square miles in size. Set on its side I calculate it would correspond in area to the counties of Kent, Surrey, Sussex, Hampshire and Berkshire, with much of Gloucestershire and Dorset as well, and would stretch from Sheerness to Bristol and from Oxford to Portsmouth. But distances count for little in Africa: forty miles is an easy hour's run on a main road, and one expects on safari to travel for three hours a day at least. The road north was not too bad: the over-laden Land Rover rode the bumps and potholes and corrugations very well, but we had covered fifty miles before we reached Mwingi, on the border of the Northern Division, and my first school was another sixteen miles further on.

It was six o'clock before we arrived at Waita. The school building, built of brick, stood perched on a rise above the group of small shops which was honoured by the name of market, and which was marked on the maps as a trading centre. Just off the road was the rest house, built by the chief for the use of government officers, a thatched mud and wattle building with two doors, one of which, on the west wall, was covered with flies basking in the warmth of the rays from the setting sun. I drove up to the rest house, climbed out of the car, stretched my legs, and helped my cook to unload.

I was carrying plenty. There was my camp bed, my bedding, my spare clothing, my food, a folding table and chair, crockery, cooking pots, books, as well as equipment for the schools, and a large tin box containing the teachers' wages. One by one the packages were lifted out on to the ground, the canvas hood of the Land Rover was lashed down for the night, and the various boxes were disposed of by the cook, some going into the rest house and some to the kitchen, a little round thatched hut some ten yards from the main building. As for myself, I walked round to the market to look for the teacher.

I found the teacher outside a tea-shop and introduced myself. He was a young man with a rather impassive face, who shook hands solemnly and walked back with me to the rest house. He said he had heard I had arrived in Kitui and had that very morning received a circular letter about the scale of school fees to be charged that year. He told me that the untrained teacher I had engaged two days before in my office had arrived with the letter, indeed had brought the letter, and was going to teach the following morning. I nodded approval of all this and was pleasantly surprised when the teacher, or headmaster as he was now, with a staff of one, suggested I could probably do with some vegetables from the school garden.

We went to inspect the garden, climbing over the stile in the thorn fence, a fence designed to keep both domestic and wild animals from eating the crops. The garden was about two acres in size, terraced and sown with maize and cow-peas and runner beans, with here and there a castor oil bush and at the far end a patch of sunflowers. It was indeed a contrast with the school gardens in my previous district in the Rift Valley. There each school had a garden sixty feet by thirty, divided neatly into eighteen plots, some of which were themselves subdivided, and on which were grown, in a pattern common to all schools in the district, up to twenty different kinds of vegetables and maize and fruit under a variety of conditions. These might be sown with or without manure, or planted either overcrowded or with proper spacing, all for the purpose of experiment and of showing the pupils what could be grown in the rich forest soil and in particular how best it could be grown. But here in Kitui, with a dry soil and with little rain, it was difficult to grow much besides maize and peas and beans, and these were grown on a large scale to feed the children who were weekly boarders at the school.

The teacher gave me two green cobs of maize and some white cow-peas. The latter were small and white, picked when the pods shrivel and the peas are quite hard. I had them with my dinner later - they were very filling and a welcome variation in my diet. I also ate a maize cob boiled - one of these is almost a meal in itself and when it is succulent and well-cooked and seasoned and eaten with butter sauce, it is worth five shillings in any London restaurant. Fortunately this was Africa: here maize may be had, if not for the asking, then at ten cobs for a shilling.

While supper was cooking I invited the headmaster to have a cup of tea, and to talk about his school and his own problems. He had been teaching for six years, and had seen the school grow from the days when it was impossible to keep more than a dozen or so boys in school throughout the year, and when girls never entered the school at all, until this year when the chief had instructed his headmen and sub-headmen to bring a hundred children to school. In fact fifty boys and thirty girls had turned up and were attending regularly every day.

This was one of the problems which I knew was awaiting me. For years the bulk of the people had taken no interest at all in education; schools were empty, the district was not producing children who could be trained as teachers, the children merely grew up in the traditional manner and followed the trades and customs of their forefathers, nothing more than subsistence farming. Then the pressure was put on; more schools were built, the benefits of education were explained to the chiefs, the propaganda machine was set to work. And now the results were appearing. The chiefs, if not the parents, became enthusiastic; the word went out, the schools were to be filled. One hundred children, two hundred, three hundred, were to be brought to school. The chiefs' henchmen went into the bush, raked out the children of school age, boys and girls, and packed them off to school. And here they were, rather bewildered, homesick, not at all sure of what the future held. Instead of a gradual development which we could cope with, a gradual increase in the school population which could be met by the opening of more schools, properly staffed with qualified teachers, we were faced with a flood of children, herded into school in the name of an ideal, a name whose magical tones were beginning to sound more and more clearly in the ears of these hitherto benighted people - *Maendeleo* - "Progress" - *Maendeleo* - "Progress". I was to hear plenty of it in the next few days. It was to be hung before my nose as a talisman. It was a reason, an excuse, a justification for pushing children into school without regard for the capacity of the schools to accept them. And with this awareness of what it meant to the people themselves - the opening of a new horizon, the raising of their existence from a very nearly futile scratching of the soil to a life of comparative ease in which due reward could nevertheless be expected for honest effort - grew the coming of hope and a belief in a happier future. I shook hands with the headmaster as he took his leave, and went back to my supper, my book, and eventually my bed, determined to have a good night's rest before facing the problems which, with no uncertainty whatsoever, the following day would bring.

I woke with the sun streaming in through the little square hole in the wall which served as a window, and pushed the mosquito net aside so that I could reach the cup of tea placed beside my camp bed by my cook. I washed, shaved and dressed, padding about in sandals on the sand floor of the rest house, and in the absence of a chair, eating my breakfast seated on an upturned box. I then collected my file of papers, told my cook to pack everything, and drove up the short road to the school.

The building was in brick with a corrugated iron roof. One wall was set six feet in from the eaves of the roof to give a broad verandah which ran very nearly the length of the building as far as the school office at one end. In front of the school were flower beds and plots of straggly grass. Beyond these was a circle of dusty ground round a flag-pole from which hung a very old Union Jack: beyond the circle, which was about fifty feet across, the ground sloped sharply down to the thorn scrub which seemed to prevail in this region. I drove round the flag-pole and parked my car in front of the office.

Inside one classroom - there were three rooms altogether but one was not in use - the headmaster was teaching. He had written on the blackboard the figures from one to ten, and was now going over thoroughly with the children the significance of the first five. He had a set of cards, showing two maize plants, five cows, three birds, one hoe, and so forth. The children were sitting, three or four to a desk, and were singing out how many things were on each card. "How many cows?" A chorus - "*Tano*" - "Five". "How many hoes?" - "*Imwe*" - "One". Then the teacher turned to the board and wrote out in large script the several figures 1, 2, 3, 4, 5. The children clenched their fists, extended their right index fingers, and carefully began to draw the figures in the air with their fingers as they said them: "Imwe, ili, itatu, inya, itano". Then repeat. And again. Then the class stood up, walked outside, squatted down on the ground by the flagpole, and with their fingers began to trace the five numbers in the dust. I watched one small girl, all seriousness, smooth the dust with a practised sweep of her palm and begin to draw. One - easy. Two - rather crooked. Three - back to front. Four - funnily enough on its side. Five - rather shaky but at least the right way round. I went round with the teacher, correcting and demonstrating, writing in the dust myself.

The children were of all sizes, from large to small. In all the schools I visited I had to send children home, much against my own will and that of the chief, but much to the relief of the teacher who was struggling often with a class of seventy. The minimum age for entering school in Kenya is seven: some of the new recruits were obviously eleven or twelve and had therefore missed their opportunity of attending school; others were small enough to be put on the waiting list for the following year, while yet others were probably only four or five. None of them could say in what year he had been born; this is a land where calendars are still rare and where family bibles are few and far between. The usually illiterate parents have no means of recording the birth of a child, and the poor school-teacher has to guess the age of his school-children as best he can when they first come to him.

Most of the boys wore shorts, some had shirts, some had both. The poorest boys had just a length of cloth wrapped round their midriff. The girls wore frocks, some of which were clearly cut from flour sacks. A few frocks were cut from plain khaki cloth ("amerikani") or from plain coloured cloth, a few from patterned cloth. Some of the girls also wore head scarves. Without exception the children were bare-footed, and would remain so for many years to come, until they began earning money of their own, or entered secondary school, where the possession of shoes was a *sine qua non* as far as personal pride was concerned. Some of the children were dirty: many were suffering from scabies which grew like a grey fungus on their heads and on the backs of their hands. These children would be treated by the doctor when he next came to the school on his rounds, and the teacher would ensure that the children would wash regularly in future and come to school clean. The scarcity of water was an ever-present problem in the district: what little could be got was needed for drinking and cooking, and washing was often a secondary consideration.

Leaving the children to carry on their work for a while on their own, the headmaster walked round the rest of the school with me. We looked again at the garden and discussed planting in the next rains. We looked at the cattle shed which needed a new roof; I promised to write to the chief and ask him to send new thatch and men to do the work. I saw the cattle which had been lent to the school by the Location Council; these provided the school with a few pints of milk a day, which was drunk by the herd boys. The cattle were lent so that the children could learn a little animal husbandry; more often than not the cattle were practically worthless as milkers or as beef producers and were in fact a good illustration of what cattle should not be like, but they gave a homely atmosphere to the school and caused welcome excitement if they broke through the fence into the garden and started to eat the growing maize. On the credit side they provided manure, and the Agricultural Officers, when they visited the school, would ensure that the sheds were kept clean and the manure properly composted.

Finally I saw the huts in which the children slept who came from a distance. Curled up on the floor and huddled together for warmth, each child with his cotton blanket, the boarders would crowd into the hut at night and, with the door shut and barred against thieves and wild animals, would sleep away the hours of darkness in some form of comfort. Supper would be maize and beans; breakfast might not happen; lunch would be more maize and beans. The chief provided as much food as he could, but there was no guarantee that the children would be well fed all the year round. Towards the end of the dry season, the maize and the beans would be infested with weevils. I suppose the children ate them, or perhaps the weevils floated out of the individual grains as the water temperature rose in the *sufuria* and were skimmed off the top of the brew. It never struck me to find out about this. But the general problem of nutrition was being tackled all the time; new crops were tried every year. In one school the teacher had been successful in growing vegetables under irrigation through water piped from a dam in the hill behind the school. In general when harvest time came, the yield was divided among the children and the plots dug over. I learned that among other things, each child in this school had been given one and a half carrots and half a tomato. The milk as I have said was drunk by the children whose job it was to milk the cows. On this first safari I came across the doctor who was District Medical Officer. He had been shocked by the discovery that the average milk yield of a cow in one location was less than a pint a day, and that once they were weaned, children received hardly any protein from their diet. In the dry districts this is still a problem which awaits solution.

I spent some time with the other teacher, who had twelve older children in his class, practising handwriting. At mid-morning break, after chatting to both teachers, I checked registers, schemes of work, records of work; and took and signed for the fees which had already been collected: every primary school child pays twenty shillings a year in fees, of which five shillings is earmarked for the buying of his own personal equipment - pencil, pen, exercise books, and so on. I paid the teachers a month's wages each, recorded my visit and made a mass of observations on it in the visitors' book, and finally, waving goodbye to children and teachers, and pausing to load my luggage and my cook into the car, I passed on up the main road to the next school on the circuit.

This was Katse. After a journey along a very stony road which twisted and turned among the hills, and which from several points gave enchanted views over the low-lying ground which sloped down to the Tana river, I found the school in full swing. The school itself was built on the same plan as that at Waita but the press of children was greater. Here there were four teachers, who seemed quite happy coping with the large number of children who had been brought in at the beginning of term: but once again I had the unpalatable task of sending children away because they were too old or too young. Among the children who were eligible to stay was a little albino boy. These children are rare - I only came across two in the whole district. Their skin

Twin Peaks, Katse Style

is very pale, with freckles or even large blotches of brown pigment, and their hair is sandy in colour: their faces are usually rather puckered and with the flat nose and fat lips they appear grotesque. Such children seem to suffer, if not the ostracism of the other children, then at least their ridicule. Although African children are normally very subdued in the presence of their elders, their instincts seem to be exactly the same as those of children elsewhere, and among themselves they can be little devils.

The only thing noteworthy about the building at Katse was its bad state of repair. I pulled at part of the doorpost of a classroom and it came away in my hand. The white ants, or termites, had eaten away the inside of the post completely, and all that remained was a painted shell. The substandard concrete floor of the verandah had cracked and in places great holes had appeared in the floor as the concrete round the cracks had crumbled away. I was to come across plenty of examples of such poor workmanship in other schools: the contracts for these schools had been put out to local builders whose cement mixtures had not been up to standard, and no check had been made on them, mainly because there was no qualified inspector in the district responsible for checking on the work done.

Doum Palms near a Village

I moved on from Katse. The road now deteriorated to a track which led first across the beds of two rivers, dry and sandy except in the rains, each some hundred feet from bank to bank. In the thick bush, one is usually quite unaware of the nearness of these rivers until the road suddenly takes a sharp turn and drops ten feet or more down a steep slope and a great expanse of sand appears ahead. The track across the sand was strewn with cut branches to prevent vehicles from becoming bogged down. The soft sand could be crossed quite easily as long as the vehicle kept moving: once it stopped in the sand, it was difficult to get it moving again, even with four-wheel drive.

Subtly the vegetation changed. Along the banks of the sand rivers the doum palm flourished to a height of thirty feet or more. Bright flowers bloomed on the trees and the baobab, the upside-down tree, with its trunk swollen to a diameter often of fifteen to twenty feet, lent an other-world appearance to the landscape. It was as if one were descending into a dream world: it became appreciably hotter as the road wound downwards into the lowland near the Tana

River, and the sunlight grew more intense. On the white sand of the river beds it shimmered with a glare that hurt the eyes, and the atmosphere became heavier as the heat increased.

The twenty mile journey from Katse took an hour and fifty minutes, during which I drove the Land Rover down sharp slopes into the beds of small streams and then up the opposite slopes crawling along in low-ratio gear, over deeply furrowed slabs of mud where a sudden storm had covered the road with silt, round rocks and over rocks, until eventually a tin roof gleamed through a clump of trees and we had reached Tharaka.

As a location, Tharaka was unique in Kitui. The name it bore was that of a tribe, the Atharaka, who spoke a language quite distinct from that of the neighbouring Akamba. Most of the Atharaka lived on the far side of the Tana River in Meru district: the Kitui Atharaka were intruders into the district, since the river marked the tribal boundary. Nevertheless they were tolerated remarkably well by the Akamba who apparently accepted them as welcome neighbours: and within the location they seemed quite happy, being ruled directly by a chief who was of their tribe. But educationally, as I found out, they had their troubles.

The headmaster, who appeared on the school doorstep to meet me, was effusive in his welcome. Benjamin was his name and in the course of the evening I heard his life history. He was an Mkamba from Katse but he spoke Kitharaka, the local language, and had been headmaster of the school since its opening six years before in 1950. During that time he had done, as far as I could see, good work; the local people thought highly of him and he was conscientious and, moreover, constantly smiling. But he had his troubles, which he soon placed before me.

The Atharaka were a small tribe, and the only book published in their language was a translation by the missionaries of the Gospel according to St. John, which seems to be the first book to be published whenever a language acquires an orthography. The reading primers in the school were all in Kikamba, and the children had no books to help them learn to read their own language. What happened was this. During the first term the children were taught in their own language, learning to read words written on the blackboard and learning to count. For the remainder of the year they learned to read and to speak Kikamba, using the readers available in the school. In the third year they began to learn Swahili, and in the fourth year, English. So in the span of the first four years in school, the education of the children embraced four languages, instead of the three in the rest of Kitui district. At the end of four years they sat a test in Kikamba and in arithmetic, all the papers being set and the answers being required in Kikamba. On the results of this test the children were selected who were to go on to Intermediate school. In the previous year only two out of some thirty entrants had gained a mark high enough to admit them to Intermediate school, and the parents and other local people felt very unhappy about it. So I promised to make allowances for the language difficulty when I marked the papers for the next test, and for the time being gave permission for all those who had failed the test but were still young enough, to stay in school for another year and sit the test again. The eventual solution was more in the nature of an experiment than anything, and I am not sure if it will work. The children were to ignore both their own language and Kikamba, and would learn to read in Swahili, and would be taught in that language from the start: in the second year they would learn English. They would be tested henceforth in Swahili. Ultimately, together with the rest of the children in the district, they would be tested in English. This pattern is followed in the (European) settled areas of the Rift Valley province, where children of different tribes, speaking different languages, attend the same school. Tuition from the start is given in Swahili, and English is begun often before the end of the first year.

I spent that night in the rest house which is one of the most pleasant and best sited in the district. It is a long building with a low wall and the thatched roof reaches almost to the ground. It is aligned east and west and at each end there is a verandah: one breakfasts in the heat of the morning sun and in the evening, over a small sundowner, watches the sun go down. To the north is the river valley: the river is a mile away and two hundred feet below. On the further bank the hills rises steeply from the river in Meru District. The scenery is on a grand scale: the hills are jagged and the cliffs rise sheer several hundred feet. After I had eaten my supper I walked out down along the path to where great slabs of rock formed a dome. I climbed to the top of this and looked out over Africa. The moon was almost full; everything was still; the hills showed dark against the sky. The air was full of the noise of crickets, a noise which is sometimes deafening and of which at other times one is not conscious at all. Far away a drum was beating, rhythmically, insistently. A fire flickered in the far distance. Everything was peaceful. When I returned to the rest house I took my shirt off because of the heat and wrote up my safari diary stripped to the waist. I was very hot in bed but I slept well once I had fallen asleep. At last I felt I was seeing the real Africa, and was as close to it as a white man and a stranger can reasonably hope to get.

The next morning I inspected the school thoroughly and went on my way. The return path took me back over my route of the day before some twenty miles where I reached the junction of the roads to Tharaka and Tseikuru. The road forks here as one approaches from Waita: I had taken the left fork to Tharaka and now I took the right fork to Tseikuru. This road was in much better condition, broad and well maintained and it was possible to cruise at thirty miles an hour much of the way. In no time we had covered the twenty-five miles to Tseikuru.

The situation here was chaotic. No other word would fit it. Three teachers - and five hundred children. Such were the ingredients of an unholy mess. The rumours which had reached me in my office a hundred miles away were true. There was evidence here of a sudden and quite unexpected enthusiasm for education which promised to embarrass everyone connected with schooling in the district and in particular me.

The facts were these. A new, young and energetic chief had been appointed four months previously. He had visited the school, discovered that the average attendance was about thirty, and had decided to put this right at once. Here was a fine building, large enough to house over a hundred children. He would find, not one hundred but two hundred, children for the school. Let it not be said that the location was backward in educating its young. For years Tseikuru had been neglected. Now was the opportunity to put it on the map. So he sent word for his headmen and his sub-headmen to foregather, which they did, and he sent them back into the *bundu* with orders to seek out every child of school age in the location and to send them to school, which they did. It is my own belief that no one was more surprised than he was when five hundred children turned up. I doubt whether many escaped the press-gang; but once the children were there the chief stuck to his guns and demanded that they all go to school. That evening he and I had a long and bitter argument about the whole matter. At least it would have been bitter had I been better able to express myself in Swahili: the argument consisted mainly of his telling me that it was my job to find teachers for these children, and in my searching somewhat fruitlessly for words in which to describe the general situation with regard to the shortage of teachers and the rules laid down by the Director of Education with regard to the maximum size of schools. The chief of course viewed with happy anticipation the posting within the week of half a dozen new teachers to the school: I on the other hand knew I could spare no trained teachers at all from the other schools in the district, and that to post untrained teachers would be courting disaster educationally. All our untrained teachers were boys of fifteen or sixteen who, after eight years in Primary and Intermediate School, had failed to win a place in High School: each had to be adequately supervised and our usual ratio in any school was two trained teachers to one untrained teacher. The calibre of the untrained teacher was sometimes high, but on one occasion I came across one who was teaching reading to a first-year class. The class were reading aloud in chorus some sentences written in Kikamba on the board, reading each sentence as the teacher pointed to it. I listened carefully for a short time, and then had to take the teacher aside and tell him quietly that although the children were reciting six sentences with verve and fluency, there were only in fact five sentences written on the board. This was rote learning at its peak.

In the end the chief agreed to send away all children who were too young or too old, but this presented difficulties. All the children seemed to be exactly the right size for entering school: some of the girls were big but our usual policy was to admit girls of any age, in order to encourage their education. And here were a hundred and sixty girls ready to be taught: it was impossible to turn them away.

A discussion with the school committee was conducted on exactly the same lines as my conversation with the chief. They sympathised with my position, agreed that the school could not cope with all the children who had turned up, and volunteered to build temporary classrooms for the children to be taught in. They were no less insistent than the chief had been that what I had to do was find the teachers.

Unloading at the new rest house in Tharaka

On the following morning I turned up as the roll was being called. The children were drawn up on the football pitch in lines. Their names were entered in exercise books pro tem: the children were divided into classes, 1a, 1b, 1c, etc., down to about 1p. The calling of the roll took about an hour and a half. I did not like to think of what was going to happen to the timetable if this had to be gone through every day.

As the children were marked off on the roll they drifted away, and I thought I had better make myself useful, so I called them together and led them under the shade of a tree which had become a temporary classroom with a blackboard propped against the trunk. I knew hardly any Kikamba, but at Waita I had learned to count up to ten, so I held up one finger and said "Imwe" - "One".

The children grasped the idea at once. We went up to ten in Kikamba, all two hundred of us. Nearly all the children seemed to be able to count, so I next went into Swahili - "*Moja, mbili, tatu ...*" - and found that most of them could count in Swahili also. Then to my great surprise I found at least a dozen boys who could count up to ten in English. So we went through my fingers in three languages and enjoyed ourselves thoroughly for about twenty minutes, when one of the teachers came along and I was relieved - in two senses.

Later I found that quite a number of the children who were enrolled as new pupils had been in school before, and these were subsequently moved up into higher classes. This explained their knowledge of English: they had spent a year or two in school but had dropped out, but the hand of Nemesis had whipped them back in again while they were still young and I think they were glad to be back, at least for a while. Perhaps economic necessity had taken them away; school fees were hard to find; goats had to be herded; or perhaps they had just grown tired of learning or had become discouraged and were happy enough to stay at home all day and play. This sort of thing happened all too often: I calculated that up to sixty per cent of children entering school in Standard One would leave within three years. In figures this meant that an intake of fifty children in Standard One would have shrunk in number to twenty by the time the children were ready to enter Standard Four.

Another problem was posed by the children who would gladly come to school for a year, and then leave usually because they were unable to pay the fees. As soon as the money was available, however, they were back in school, and stayed there until times grew hard again, when off back home they would go. Sometimes they would go back to school and repeat a class, if they had forgotten what they had learned earlier: sometimes they would be promoted to the next class even after a year's absence, and would have to try to recall was they had previously been taught as best they could. I had already come across this phenomenon of broken schooling and I had painful memories of the experience, which I think are worth repeating here.

The previous year when I was working as District Education Officer in the Rift Valley, I had to collect and summarise statistics for children in school. Among the information called for was the length of time the children had been in school - so many children with one year's schooling, so many with two, and so on, down to about fifteen years. This sounds easy enough - each child counts the years back to the time he first entered school and puts his hand up when the teacher calls out that particular number. The teacher writes down the hand count and sends it to me, along with the number of children in each class. I quickly found out that the two sets of numbers did not tally even closely, which seemed to me to be wrong. I composed a short sharp circular giving concise instructions as to how to assess this information and sent it out to all schools. As an additional move I went personally to visit one school whose headmaster has obviously misunderstood completely what he had to do.

I arrived at the school and, having summoned the headmaster and told him what I intended to do, I marched him into Standard III and addressed the class.

I soon ran into difficulties. What I had not understood myself was that all the children had parents who were liable to move from place to place and that many children had been in this particular primary school only for a short time. The first conversation went like this.

"You, boy, stand up. What is your name?"
"Nderitu, sir."
"Well, Nderitu, you are now in Standard III?"
"Yes, sir."
"What standard were you in last year?"
"I wasn't in school last year, sir."
"Oh." A pause. "Well, were you in school the year before?"
"Yes, sir, in Nyeri." (In Central Province.)
"Good. What standard were you in then?"
"I think I was in Standard III, sir."
"And the year before that?"
A pause. "I wasn't in school."
"But were you ever in Standard II?"
"Yes, sir."
"When?"
"I don't know, sir."
"Was it four years ago?"
"I don't know."
"Was it in 1952 or 1953?"
"I don't know."
"When were you in Standard I?"

"I don't know."

"When did you first go to school?"

"I think it was in 1948 but I don't know."

I turned to the headmaster who was looking impassive. "But if this boy started school in 1948, he has been in school on and off for seven years."

The headmaster raised his eyebrows in assent.

"But he can't be more than ten now. That would make him only three years old when he entered school."

The headmaster continued to look impassive.

I looked at the other children. They too looked impassive.

The headmaster and I looked at each other. Then with a wild look in my eye, I shook hands silently with the headmaster, turned to the door, walked out to my Land Rover and drove back to my office where I sat down and began to make the necessary and totally fictitious alterations to the results for the school population figures to balance, and so satisfy my superiors in Nairobi.

Before I left Tseikuru, having given way to the chief for at least the time being, and having promised to send another teacher to help deal with the mob, I was privileged to witness a small scene which was most significant from the viewpoint of education as an economic matter. As I was sitting in the school office writing comments in the visitors' book (if I remember correctly, I began my remarks with the word "Wow!"), a woman came along the verandah. She was dressed in the long strip of black cloth wrapped round the waist and carried up over the shoulder, which is worn by those woman who have not yet come under the influence of the mission sewing class. On her back she carried a basket supported by a strap which was passed across her forehead; a gaily coloured headscarf covered her hair, and by the hand she led a little boy quite naked except for a string of beads round his neck. He was about three years old and rather overawed by the school building: he stood with his thumb in his mouth, his eyes round and liquid.

The headmaster came out to the woman who dug down into the folds of the black cloth and drew out a crumpled twenty-shilling note which had once been yellow and which was now a muddy tan colour. A long conversation followed, conducted with politeness yet with insistence on the woman's part. It could by no means be called an argument, but the headmaster at last clearly prevailed, took the twenty shillings, and wrote a receipt which he gave to the woman. She with a resigned countenance tucked the receipt into her clothing, turned, and wandered off with the little boy in tow. I asked the headmaster what had happened.

It seemed that the woman was most upset. She had three children; a little girl of about eight, the little boy of three whom I had seen, and a baby of a month or so. Now the chief had sent for the eldest child to go to school, and had thereby disturbed the happy economic equilibrium of the family. Normally, while the mother dug and tended the family plot, the girl would care for the baby. Now with the girl in school, there was no one to look after the baby, and the mother's work was suffering. Please would the headmaster send the girl back home where she was badly needed: in her place we could have the three-year-old boy. The answer had had to be "No", and I realised that the post of headmaster in these little schools carried a greater burden of worry and needed far more tact and firmness than I had imagined.

The incident illuminated another noteworthy fact in the district. In the outlying locations, enthusiasm for education emanated from the chief alone, and the parents generally would be indifferent or even hostile to his attempts to herd the children into school. Children who ran away from school would be brought back by the tribal police and punished, but the parents would often take no side in the matter. There were even parents who paid the school fee and immediately took their children away from school to herd goats or cattle. When they were upbraided for this, they would reply: "We have paid you the school fee. What more do you want?" and yet fifty miles away near the townships, children were being turned away from school for lack of room. Those Africans who were pressing for further expansion in the school system to meet the demand for places were usually unaware of the indifference to schooling shown by the more backward people in the outer locations, and found it hard to believe me when I told them of it. They themselves had seen only the schools in the Central Division where many of the parents had themselves been educated and wished their children also to go to school. The fact was that in ten locations in Kitui children were kept in school by force, and in the other thirteen locations children were being turned away from school. In 1957 I calculated that over the district as a whole more than half the children applying to go school had to be turned away. In one school two hundred children turned up for admission to a first year class which could only take forty-eight. But the District Education Board agreed that the social services in the outer locations must not be allowed to lag behind those in the central locations, and of four new primary schools to be opened in 1957, three were allocated to the outer locations and only one new one was to be built in the Central Division. The current enthusiasm for learning has come ten years too late. Had it appeared at the end of the war when money was available for spending, the school system by now would have been twice its present size. But money is now tight, economies have to be made, and indeed for a time it looked as if development would have to stop altogether for several years. In the future it seems unlikely that the system will expand sufficiently to meet demand, unless money appears in great quantities, both for the equipping of schools and for the training of many more teachers.

[The picture shows a new Intermediate school under construction at Ikutha, with a corrugated iron roof. The bricks are baked locally in great kilns fired with wood.]

I came in the course of my safaris to take nothing for granted. One day I would visit a school to find a fine building with glazed steel windows, doors which locked, children who were neatly dressed, books which were up-to-date and well cared for. The children wrote in cheap exercise books, but these were clean and tidy and were obviously well looked after and valued. On the following day I would drive thirty miles further into the bush and find a little mud and wattle hut with leaky thatch: on rough benches squatted muddy children clutching bits of broken slate in one hand and stubs of slate pencil in the other. The teacher wrote on an white-ant-eaten blackboard: very often there was little light in the hut, the reading books in the school were torn and smeared with grime and very often had no covers and a reduced complement of pages. Fortunately this type of school was nearly extinct: a clean-up campaign by the Education Officer in the past few years had succeeded in getting chiefs to build well-constructed schools using baked brick, funded often with money collected from the people living locally.

But there are even now still too many schools with dilapidated buildings. Many were built with only three walls which is an excellent design when the weather is hot, since it gives plenty of light and ventilation, and since it also has a roof is one step better than having the school meet under a tree, whereas the old-type windowless hut is any number of steps worse. But in the rainy season, when the damp mists drift in the hilly country, the lack of a fourth wall is felt very keenly.

I must pause a minute to recall the sound of two dozen slate pencils squeaking over two dozen slates. It had been my impression until I came to Kenya that slates went out with the bustle, or at least with the coming of the Board Schools in Britain, but here in Kenya they were not only still being used but were being replaced with new ones when they disintegrated. It was a revelation to see a child's face when after sorting through a huge pile of slate fragments in the bottom of a cupboard in search of a piece large enough to write on, he was given a brand new one by the teacher. Clean white-wood frame, shining grey-black centre, it seemed almost a sacrilege to deface it with the scribbles of a slate pencil. However the slate has always had the advantage over paper in the matter of erasing. A finger dampened with the tongue - and the ungraceful letter is wiped off and the word completed to the satisfaction of the pupil. And when the whole slate is full it can be wiped clean with a sweep of the shirt sleeve or the hem of the skirt. And if this is too straightforward and unexciting a way of doing it, then the writer dribbles copiously on to the slate and holds the slate at an angle, this way and that, while the dribble makes intricate patterns of black on the grey of the slate before being wiped clean. As I watched African children in these and other diversions, I came to the conclusion that in their delight in simple pleasures they are exactly the same as other children everywhere.

[African and other dark-skinned children have an advantage over pale-skinned children in one particular. Mathematical calculations can be done with a pencil on the inside of the forearm - on the dark skin the pencil makes light but easily read scratches, which can be rubbed off with a damp finger when the calculation is finished with.]

Watoto (see page 90)

Shanzu Beach Hotel

Here is a piece of the shore of the Indian Ocean, and this particular piece goes with the Shanzu Beach Hotel, near Mombasa, where I spent Christmas 1954 with friends. Beyond the trees is the beach, composed of white coral sand, and beyond that is the ocean, calm and blue. Just below the horizon is the white line of surf marking the barrier reef of coral, which helps to keep the sharks, as in sharks-fin soup, off the beach. Bathing was done in usual bathing dress, supplemented by a shirt to ward off the sunburn, and by old plimsoles to ward off the medical condition known as "nasty holes in the feet",

caused by standing on spiny sea urchins, which abound in the shallow water. At this time of day the bathers are off the beach, having a siesta, resting up from their exertions of the morning, exertions which include getting outside a sizeable lunch and a drink or two (or three).

In the lower picture we see the verandah of the afore-mentioned hotel. The little blobs which look like upside-down half-coconuts hanging from the palm trees are weaver birds' nests. The flappy objects on the near right are the bathers' towels drying, while it looks as if someone has discarded a pair of shoes on the verandah. Neither of the retreating figures in the middle distance is me.

Although Shanzu was a cut below the nearby Nyali Beach Hotel, the choice of the wealthy, our hotel was easy-going and friendly, an ideal place in which to enjoy a Merry Christmas, or, in the local argot, "Melly Kissy-missy".

KILIMANJARO

In 1956, through my involvement with the Scout movement in Kenya, I was invited to be part of the leadership team running an Outward Bound course for young men, selected from all races in the Colony. Needless to say, I accepted the invitation and spent three weeks of my local leave preparing for and attempting successfully an ascent of Kilimanjaro, at 19,300 feet Africa's highest mountain.

A few weeks later, I sat down and typed out some memories of the course. The base camp was a former African Primary School, taken over by the Outward Bound Trust. The training programme was designed to allow the young men, or "boys" as it seems simpler to refer to them, to become fit and to learn some of the skills of living in the wilderness. The base was at Loitokitok, a Masai name meaning "The Place of Bubbling Waters", still on the grassy plains of the Rift Valley. Close by was the forest, and higher up were the lower slopes of the mountain, noted first for stunted trees hung with long strands of lichen, and after that for giant heather and little else in the way of vegetation. Here the first cave was located, a great overhang of rock under which twenty people could sleep in the dry if not in comfort. At this stage of the journey, streams of ice-cold water ran down the slopes and drinking water was plentiful. A little higher up, there were no streams, and by this point filled water bottles had to be carried and water conserved.

A few more miles further on the saddle began, slung between the twin peaks of Mawenzi, an old eroded volcanic core, and Kibo, the newer crater with gases still escaping from the dormant magma beneath. Here the second cave was located. The saddle was ten thousand feet up and little grew on it except everlasting flowers. At the point at which the steep slopes of Kibo joined the saddle, earlier mountaineers had built a small hut, with bunks for a couple of

71

dozen people and precious little spare space else inside.

It was from this hut that each final climb began, starting at three in the morning when it was bitterly cold—too cold to move but too cold to stand still, a nasty dilemma—and the ground was still frozen. The slopes of Kibo were covered in loose scree, and climbing was a simple matter of putting one foot after the other, with firm ground beneath until the sun rose at six o'clock and the ice began to melt. Here the air was thin, breathing was difficult, and progress was slow. On a later ascent I suffered from mountain sickness, for no apparent reason. At the right time of the year the sky above would be blue, with clouds below around the lower slopes.

The first point reached on the summit was Gilman's Point, with a cross and a tin box with a book in it for climbers to write their names in as proof they had got there. It was possible to walk right round the rim of the crater but only if the snow conditions made it safe to do so. Climbers starting from Arusha in what was then Tanganyika, also arrived at Gilman's Point on their climb.

Coming down was easy, a matter of running down the scree, and then walking down the saddle and the lower slopes and down through the forest to the base. Relief to be home and joy at having made the ascent.

Six months later I used my experience of the mountain to lead a small party of young people from the American Mission at Kijabe in the Rift Valley as far as the summit and back. There were no problems.

On this first ascent sixteen young men, their ages ranging from 16 to 22, tramped along in single file. Each carried on his back some thirty or forty pounds weight of equipment. Underneath the tramping feet the ground was almost bare of vegetation: hard rock alternated with soft gravel. Apart from isolated clumps of everlasting flowers and a little heather, the place around seemed devoid of all life. There were no animals, no birds, There was no sound except the tread of feet, the occasional clink of a nail against rock, and the laboured breathing of the members of the party. Without preamble, a command came from the end of the line, where one of the four instructors was encouraging the stragglers.

"Ten minutes."

Trekking across the saddle

The line broke up. The leaders stopped abruptly, and as the rest caught up with them, all swung their packs off their backs, eased their shoulders, grunting a little, and selected a rock on which to sit or against which to lean. Some were too weary even to remove their packs, and sat down with their packs still on, and leaned back on them. One boy removed a boot to inspect a blistered foot; hands dipped into pockets and brought out sweets or chocolate; one of the instructors produced a needle and twine and set about mending a strap which had broken loose from his rucksack. One of the boys moved a short distance away and took a photograph of the party. Several of the boys thought of the full water bottles which added to the weight of the packs. Despite the fact that the party had been marching for nearly four hours, the leader would allow no one to drink. Water was precious; the party would not find water again for twenty-four hours, and discipline was necessarily rigid.

The landscape was not inviting. Here, at 14,000 feet, with driving mist hiding much of the scene, the prospect was one of red and yellow and grey rock, loose scree thrown down from the flanks of the mountain by wind and by water, and the whole rising gently, exasperatingly, as far as the horizon. Hidden in the mist behind the party as it sat in the midst of this great waste was the snow-covered summit of Kibo, the great truncated cone of Kilimanjaro; before them, swathed in cloud, lay the jagged peak of Mawenzi. At the end of their path lay the little hut which, crouched at the foot of the slopes of Kibo, was to shelter the party that night.

"Saddle up!"

With wry smiles and further grunts, the party obeyed. Packs were swung onto shoulders again, sticks or ice-axes were taken in hand, and the procession re-formed and moved off. At the front one of the instructors followed the faint trail left by the party which had gone ahead on the previous day. Every few yards the mark of a nailed boot showed in the gravel

Ten minutes' rest

and satisfied the leader that the party were headed in the right direction.

A shout from one of the party caused each of the others to look up and to forget momentarily the weight of his pack. The mist had lifted for a moment and far ahead up the slope could be seen a group of moving figures. The first party was on its way down.

Soon the two parties were within hailing distance of each other, the one still slogging doggedly uphill, the other coming down almost at a trot, with the hardship of walking uphill finally behind them. The parties met and amalgamated. The instructors gathered together and exchanged notes. The scree was very loose towards the top; the snow was fresh and treacherous; the journey round from Gilman's point to Kaiser Wilhelm Spitz was not to be attempted; in the second cave down on the moorland, there was so much food for the first party to use, so much to be left for the second party; of the nineteen members of the first party, all but one had reached the summit. Around the group of instructors, the boys were discussing their own experiences and giving their own views on the scree and on the snow and the weather.

Another command, and the two parties formed up, ready to go their separate ways. The one continued on its slow climb, heartened now by the knowledge that the hut lay at the end of less than an hour's march; the other swept on its way down the mountain to where in the second cave were stored the butter, golden syrup, bottles of orange squash and tins of pineapple which were to be the consolation for withstanding the rigours of a very strict rationing during the previous two days.

This party also did the upward-bound party a good turn by enticing away the grey-haired shenzi bitch who, wearing a collar of ticks, may very well have set a canine (and tick) altitude record by reaching this height. The dog normally lived somewhere near the school in Loitokitok and subsisted on scraps from the school kitchen. She had come in the past fortnight to associate food and its supply with the presence of the young thugs who one morning packed up and disappeared down the road. Naturally she picked up our trail and followed us. Nothing we had tried, and we had tried most things short of violence, would induce her to turn back and she had followed us faithfully through the forest, across the moor with its giant heathers and into this barren place. It was with a good deal of relief that we saw her capering about at the heels of the other party as they faded away into the mist.

The Kibo Hut – Not much to look at but it's Home

The going became harder as the angle of the slope increased, and some of the boys began to lag. The line strung out. Then, just a small shining speck among the rocks up onto our left, the little tin hut of Kibo came into view. Some of the party quickened their pace and went off almost at a gallop to reach the hut and to have a drink of water; others were glad to relax a little and to slow down now that the goal was so near. All of them reached it finally and preparations began for the ascent of the summit on the following day.

* * * * * * *

The boys were members of the eighth Outward Bound course to be held in Kenya. Most of them were still at school. Of the few who had left school—and the school-leaving age in Kenya could be as late as twenty—some were working and others were training as teachers. Of the thirty-one on the course, fourteen were African, ten were European and seven were Asian. Already they were working as a team, and were beginning to forget differences of birth and culture in the communal life.

The instructors were chosen for their experience of living rough and of coping with life in the wilderness. Three of us had come up through the ranks of the Scout movement, a tough training which had equipped us to be resourceful and self-sufficient and capable of surviving in extreme conditions, and, which was of greater importance here, to be able to train others in the same skills and to be able to sustain the well-being of those others in any emergency. Another was an Army officer with similar training.

The ascent of Kibo was to be the climax of the three-week course, and the previous two weeks had been taken up with preparations for the main exercise. Yet the scaling of the mountain was not the excuse for the course. The presence of the mountain was very convenient, and climbing it would be a fine test, with problems to be solved and hardships to be endured, but a test which the organisers would be free and able to dispense with if they so desired. The boys would be expected to say afterwards: "I have been on an Outward Bound course", rather than: "I have climbed Kilimanjaro".

It will be seen therefore that, although it was the aim of each boy to reach the summit, his failure to do so would not mean that the remainder of the course would be of no value to him. Several who reached Gilman's Point failed in the other activities which the course embraced. Some of these failures were physical—a failure to reach a set standard in the long jump or in running the quarter-mile. Other failures were more serious—a failure to keep one's temper, to keep cheerful—these indicated weaknesses of personality. On the other hand those few who did not reach the top of the mountain nevertheless showed themselves to be very sound in such things as keeping in good humour and being fair-minded and tolerant. All these things were observed and noted by the instructors who, at the end of the course, prepared a report on each boy's behaviour and progress during the course. This report was sent later to the boy's headmaster or employer.

* * * * * * *

The preparations for this final exercise had been well thought out and well executed. The adventures of my own patrol in the early days of the course may give some idea of the sort of thing which was designed to train the boy in the art of self-reliance.

We began by studying the intricacies of the magnetic compass. The mathematically-minded among us found no difficulty in understanding the theory of taking a bearing and a back-bearing, and most of the boys were able after ten minutes to take a fairly accurate bearing on Mawenzi whose snow-slashed peak was visible from the base camp on most mornings. The setting of a map and the marching on a bearing were things which we soon had an opportunity of putting into practice. The next morning every boy shouldered a fairly light rucksack containing various assorted pieces of equipment, and the whole patrol went off, down through the town of Loitokitok and into the bush country to the north. The intention was for us all to march on a set bearing for so long, then to turn along the second side of an equilateral triangle, and finally for us all to find our way back to the base. We took a compass bearing and as luck would have it a large euphorbia tree lay in exactly the right direction. We walked the quarter-mile to the tree and then everyone sat down and tried to remove the sharp grass seeds which were sticking into his socks. After this had been proved by experiment and argument to be impossible, the patrol set off again, this time with no tree conveniently growing in the line of march. One boy walked with a compass in his hand, trying to keep the party going in the right direction, while the others sought ways of getting through the thorn thickets which seemed to be the only kind of life supported on the plains.

A diversion occurred when Stephen, an African schoolboy from Machakos, shot off at a tangent and wound up in front of a bush on which were growing brightly coloured berries. These were the size of very small plums and varied in colour from a deep red to an orange-yellow. Stephen, who had spent his early years herding goats, asserted that these things were edible, and eventually we believed him and followed his example and ate some ourselves. Most of the rest of the trip we spent in looking out for more of these fruits.

When we considered we must be well out into the wilderness, we happened on a strip of ground which had been cleared of bush and which proved to be Loitokitok airstrip. This rather disappointed us and we decided it was time to turn on to the second leg of the triangle. As soon as the mathematicians, with great laying of sticks on the ground and writing on the backs of envelopes, had decided on the new bearing, we resumed our journey, which was thereafter uneventful save for an unsuccessful sortie in which the hunters in the patrol tried to kill half a dozen guinea fowl for the pot by throwing sticks and stones at them.

The value of this morning trip lay most of all in the carrying of the rucksacks. All gear had to be carried up the mountain by the boys themselves and it was vital that they get used to carrying heavy packs on their backs. Two days later, therefore, the patrol set out again, with heavier packs and with food for a mid-day meal. This time the route led uphill, along the course of a stream which flowed down out of the forest.

The first part of the journey lay along fairly well-marked paths. It was cool in the forest and the going was easy. Several times the stream had to be forded or crossed by stepping stones; once again, just as we thought we must be stepping where no man had stepped before, we came to evidence of precursors—a road and a large clearing where the timber company had been cutting trees for a number of years. This was the most difficult country to walk through; the bush had grown thick in the clearing and it was a question very often of forcing a path through close-growing coppice. The boys managed very well however and we soon arrived on the edge of the forest again. We paused beneath a picturesque cedar growing beside the stream, ate our biscuits, and drank our fill of water. The pure mountain water was to be our main drink in our trip up to the summit, and there is no doubt of its superiority over the stuff which comes out of a well or through a tap. It has a flavour which is not readily forgotten and even after it has been kept for a day or two in a water bottle, it still tastes sweet and fresh.

Cooking Lunch in the Forest

We were still in thick forest and learning to recognise and avoid the stinging nettles before we walked into them, when lunch-time came. A spot was chosen beside the stream and a pair of fires was lit. Two sufurias were filled from the stream and set on the fires to boil. Then began the ritual of preparing the main dish. As the water came to the boil, the rice was added; then came the macaroni, the carrots and the potatoes. When all these were cooked through, a tin of corned beef was opened and its contents broken up into the stew. The meal was then served up to the patrol and for a little while there was comparative silence in the forest. Cocoa and biscuits were the second and only other course. The fires were put out and the plates were washed, and the patrol turned back to find its way down through the forest and back to base at the school. The return was much easier than the outward journey had been, indeed it was completed in two hours, whereas the morning's trip had taken three. The big event on the return journey was the sighting of a particularly large elephant on the opposite side of the stream, a short way up the hill. It seemed too engrossed in eating branches to be interested in us.

Later we were to see and hear more elephant in the forest, and all the paths we followed were punctuated by elephant droppings. When we were about a mile from the base, I dropped a word into the ear of the hindmost member of the patrol; shortly afterwards he sat down on the ground and appeared to be in considerable pain I called back the rest of the patrol and pointed out how it was clearly impossible for Ferdnand to walk the remaining distance to the base. Fortunately the patrol had been shown only the day before how to make a stretcher from a climbing rope, and equally fortunately we happened to be carrying a climbing rope with us. A stretcher was made and for the next twenty minutes young Ferdnand was carried in comfort up a narrow path by six other boys, each carrying thirty pounds on his back as well as his share of Ferdnand. The remarkable recovery of Ferdnand immediately after he had been laid gently on his mattress in the dormitory was not unexpected by one or two of the cannier members of the patrol, but the others, when they realised that their efforts had not been entirely in a good cause, were at first bewildered and then angry and had to be held down. The operation showed clearly however that anyone who was unwise enough to break a leg on the mountain was likely to be unpopular. But bearing in mind a recent tragedy among mountaineering circles in Kenya, the exercise and the practice were necessary.

The rest of the training was carried on continuously. Every morning there were exercises before breakfast. Every day the boys could practise on the ropes course. There were lectures given on mountain rescue, on ropework, on the use of a primus stove, and on the general care of kit. One instructor, a geologist by training, gave one evening an illustrated lecture on the geology of the mountain which aroused a good deal of interest among the boys. Lantern slides were shown illustrating such varied things as life on the Falkland Islands, the Outward Bound courses held in Great Britain and

Still cooking

Washing up

the sights an American sees when he tours Europe and East Africa. As for the daily life at the base camp, perhaps a few brief glimpses will serve to capture its spirit.

*   *   *   *   *   *   *

As I lay in bed and watched the sky grow lighter, from deep indigo through the infinite shades of blue and green, everything was still. A light breeze only stirred the branches of the cypress trees which lined the road leading past the school. From the kitchen where breakfast was being prepared, there came the occasional sound of an iron spoon meeting an iron pot. Suddenly there was a splash, and another, then a third. The surface of the little swimming pool was lashed by flailing arms and legs and the sound of splashing woke the late sleepers, who shivered as they hunted around for socks and shoes. So did I shiver as I thought of those bygone days when I could bring myself to indulge in such Spartan activity, and I envied the three boys who could bear to bathe at that ungodly hour of the day.

*   *   *   *   *   *   *

"Seconds up!" A queue formed by the hatchway, hungry boys of all colours but with one appetite. The amount of food they seemed able to assimilate was prodigious, and it says a lot for the cooks that there was little food ever left to be thrown away. Indeed after being caught out on one or two occasions, the cooks used to help themselves before serving the food up to the boys. As the boys sat round finishing their porridge or stew or, it might well be, their macaroni cheese, one meditated on the variety of diet which these boys would be eating when they returned home. For many it was their first ever acquaintance with marmalade. Few of the European boys would have been used to eating goat meat, which they all voted very palatable. One African boy admitted that he was very homesick and was longing to get outside a good meal of maize and beans when he got home. Before the end of the course, however, he was converted to macaroni cheese. (Converted "to", not "into"!) I do not know whether he will try and expand his diet in the future, but it seems to me that it would be a shame if he were not to follow up some of the foods he was introduced to on this course and at least occasionally add them to his beans and maize. It was a week spent in Paris as a student that first gave me a taste for exotic cheese and black coffee. So it may well be a course such as this that adds goat to the European table, and to the African or Asian table cheese and marmalade and suet pudding.

*   *   *   *   *   *   *

The young Asian boy had never climbed a tree before in his life, let alone a rope. Gingerly he made his way up this particular tree, using old knot holes and the stumps of branches as hand-and foot-holds. He reached the place where the rope was tied to the tree and stepped on to the knot. Keeping his eyes on the foot-rope, he felt with his hands for the hand-rope above his head. When he had found this, he moved his other foot on to the lower rope and began slowly, one foot, one hand, the other foot, the other hand, to sidle along the rope bridge. The hand rope was slack and came down level with his face. If his feet were to go forward, he would swing over on to his back, and the ground was ten feet below. With grim concentration he progressed until his foot met the knot at the far end of the bridge. Now he could grasp the branch of the other tree, which to him was as welcome as the firm ground. He had overcome the first physical obstacle on the course.

*   *   *   *   *   *   *

Tomas, the young Polish boy, looked down at the ground twenty feet below. From where he was in the tree, it looked a long way down. He was expected now to jump out into space from the branch on which he was standing, and put his whole trust in the piece of rope he had wound round his wrists. This rope was attached by a karabiner, a snap-link, to the main rope which ran down to the base of another tree growing some distance away. This main rope was not very tight, and it was not easy to take up the slack when you were standing in the tree. It therefore took a fair amount of courage to leap into space for the first time with no immediate support. or indeed for the second or third time, for that matter.

Tomas wound up his courage, as we all did when we made the same leap, and jumped. He fell a few feet, then the slack took up and took the weight of his fall. Instead of falling, he began to slide sideways, faster and faster, revolving slowly as he did so, until his feet met the ground. He spun round so that he was going backwards, and came to rest on a grassy bank, sitting on his backside. He too had overcome his obstacle.

*   *   *   *   *   *   *

Hudson, a great six-footer from Nyanza, lowered himself on to the single rope stretched twenty feet above the ground. Lying face down on the rope, with one foot hooked back over it and the other leg hanging free to lower his centre of gravity and balance his body, he began to haul himself along the rope with his hands. When he reached the middle of the rope he paused, then allowed himself to swing down off the rope so that he was hanging by his arms. With a heave he hooked his ankles back over the rope, with another he pulled his body up and got an elbow over the rope as well. Then, kicking down vigorously with one leg, he rolled over the rope on to his stomach, regained his balance, and hauled himself along to the far end of the rope where the next problem was waiting to be solved.

* * * * * * *

One of the more spectacular problems of the many included in the course was an indoor one. It was called the "table traverse". The table was a large one with a leg at each corner, and measured some seven feet by three feet and a half. Each patrol in turn had three minutes in which to get as many of its members as possible under the table and up the other side, in the manner traditionally associated with a Cossack passing under his horse's stomach. No part of the body was to touch the ground.

Each boy lay on the table face downwards. Then without touching the ends of the table or its legs, the boy swung over one edge, reached under the table with one arm for the other edge, transferred one foot also to the other edge, and hung there suspended looking in all the world like a three-toed sloth. This part was relatively easy. The difficult part followed. The boy had to transfer his weight on to one arm, which he tried to get as far as possible on to the table top. If he hung down too far the table would overbalance and fall on top of him. No one was allowed to hold the table while the boy was trying the traverse. By inching his way on one elbow back on to the top of the table, the boy could eventually grasp the

Near the Second Cave

far edge and pull himself over on to the top. It says a lot for the sense of balance of many of the boys that a third of them succeeded in this very difficult manoeuvre. The sense of balance needed here was needed later when, near the second cave on the mountain, the whole party spent an afternoon rock-climbing.

* * * * * * *

The most intensive training for the climb to the summit took the form of a climb on the lower slopes of the mountain as far as the second cave, at ten thousand feet. Only the effort of slogging up through the forest, along a path which very often was little more than a stone staircase, and with a thirty or forty pound pack on one's back, could have prepared the boys for the long climb up to the summit. The ostensible object of the three-day trip to the second cave was to deposit stores, but it served very well also as a test of boots, muscles and tempers. As far as boots went, very few of the boys had really suitable boots for climbing or for marching. Many of the party wore rubber-soled shoes as far as the hut, and wore their nailed boots only for the final climb. Muscles of course were aching all the time, and one was constantly discovering new muscles which took on the torch from the original muscles which had just about settled down to do an uncomplaining job of work. And tempers frayed rather too easily at times. But the impression one got from the talk, especially back at the base, was that it was all rather good fun.

79

* * * * * * *

I do not know for certain in what light those boys who took part in the course looked back on it later. I do know that at least one boy said he would like to come back as an instructor on another course. I imagine that most remembered it with great pleasure for despite its hardships, the atmosphere was nearly always one of cheer and good humour. There was always something to laugh about, just as there was always something to complain about, and on balance the laughter drowned the complaints. And there was always something which threw a challenge at the boys, something which possibly could have been avoided. I recall a Punch cartoon from many years ago, possibly by David Langdon, showing a group of soldiers undergoing battle training. They were confronted with a fifteen foot high wall topped with several strands of barbed wire, and the sergeant in charge was saying: "Now I dare say that normally the tendency would be to go *round* this sort of thing". I think it was fair to say that there was very little noticeably circumvention on this course. The determination to succeed usually triumphed. Speaking for myself, the greatest temptation I have ever faced was the temptation to turn back when I was some thousand feet below the summit.

* * * * * * *

* * * * * * *

In the hut we woke at two on a starlit night. The moon was coming up as we crawled out of our sleeping bags, fully dressed except for boots and wind-proof jackets. A brew of black coffee and a brace of biscuits and butter lined our stomachs for the day's work ahead. Boots were put on and laced and tied with care. Cameras were loaded with film, balaclava helmets were adjusted to protect as great an area of our faces as possible. At three we were ready to go.

The Path Upward

Our first casualty happened after an hour's climbing—sore legs. An instructor had to return with the boy to the hut. After another half hour another boy complained of feeling sick and dizzy, and he too had to be escorted back. The party strung out, climbing ever upwards, ever more slowly. I stayed at the rear to watch over the stragglers. Eventually as dawn sent a pale light over the eastern horizon and the summit above us shone white against an indigo sky, two more of the boys had to turn back. One could get no grip with his shoes on the hard snow which we had just reached: the other was just cold and tired. He could barely move down the mountain again, and could certainly have gone no further up the slope. I left the party in the charge of my assistant and began the journey back to the hut. By the time there was light and the path could be seen, we had descended a thousand feet. Then we met the instructor who had gone back with the first casualty, on his way up again. He persuaded me to turn round and begin climbing again and rejoin the others: the hut was now in sight so we left the two boys to wander slowly back on their own.

Myself at the summit of Kibo

The next three hours were hard. I was myself beginning to tire, and by the time we were in reach of the summit, I knew something of what those boys had experienced who had turned back. I think all of us must have felt the same: the climb became a real struggle. It was ten paces on, a collapse on to a rock or even on to the snow, and a rest of five minutes, until one was breathing fairly easily again and the heart-beat rate was back to somewhere below a hundred. At first one could manage to enjoy the beauty of the scene. The sun lit up the ridges in a red blaze, and the snow shone with a glare which forced us to put on our snow goggles. To our left the ice-wall of the snow cap stood out sharply against the sky which at this altitude was a deep violet, shading off into blue towards the horizon. All around, five thousand feet below us, lay a swelling carpet of white cloud. Eventually the beauty of the scene ceased to register, and the one thought in all minds was the struggle upwards. It was only the sight of figures walking about on the summit far above us that gave us the will to try to reach the top. Added to the state of exhaustion which all of us were now in was the thought of the vertiginous slope up which we were walking. To look back was a terrifying experience. As for me, I found myself wondering how easy it might be to fall over and roll down the slope, over and over into the abyss below us…

But at last the top was within reach. The party who had reached the summit before us had come up by another path and had gone back the same way, so we did not meet them on their way down. We could only find out who had reached the top by reading the names written in the book kept in a tin box at the summit at Gilman's Point. For a while we rested, gazing at the indescribable glories of the snow scenes in the crater itself. I took a photograph of Mawenzi from underneath an arm of the cross which stands on the summit, and someone took a photograph of me with the ice wall as a background.

At Gilman's Point

The sun was melting the ice which held the scree together, and it took us only half an hour to run back down the path which we had spent five hours in climbing up. The pain we had suffered we quickly forgot. But pain it had been. It was certainly the toughest physical test that I had ever faced and I am certain that all the boys would have said the same for themselves. To climb Kilimanjaro with porters is one thing; to carry all your own gear on your back is another. And all but seven of the thirty-nine souls in the party reached the top. Those who did not lacked nothing in determination. In fact the determination to win through and the degree of perseverance shown by some of these boys was at times almost an embarrassment to the instructors. Frequently they had to order a boy to stop trying something which was obviously beyond his powers, and some of these orders were by no means readily obeyed.

The return to base camp was easy. A night at the second cave, with unlimited fresh water to drink and to bathe in, although the temperature of streams fed by ice-melt has to be felt to be believed. The clearing up at the base, with the towering flames of the camp fire illuminating healthy, happy, singing faces on the last night. Goodbye to Gene, a visitor from the United States, who went to sleep halfway up the mountain; goodbye to Gilbert, the geologist, who threw away his prospector's hammer on a steep snow slope as unwanted ballast and who had it presented to him again by a member of the second party who found it on the following day, sticking out of the snow; goodbye to Paul, incredibly fit, who made the climb from the hut to the summit of Kibo in two and a half hours, and accompanied our singing on the mouth-organ. Goodbye to Donald who, with the illogicality of his race (for these words he would never forgive me) carried his bag-pipes to the summit and startled the silent places into echo. And goodbye to all those of many colours and creeds who were for three weeks our friends, companions and confidants. It was all great fun and very worthwhile.

And a final word. No undertaking as ambitious as this can be seen through successfully without adequate leadership. The success of this project was due almost entirely to the work of Major Dacre Stroud, Principal of the Kenya Outward Bound School at Loitokitok. He combined faultless planning with a modest but firm air of authority, trusting in his instructors and having the welfare of every participant at heart. As long as men of his calibre can be found, the work of bringing young people to an understanding and fulfilment of their own potential will continue. Thank you, Dacre.

Ready to travel back to Nairobi. Major Dacre Stroud is in the right foreground

Pages from My Diary

(You've seen the pictures before)

Here are the Outward Bound boys trekking up on to the saddle between Kibo and Mawenzi.

They have lost interest by now in picking the flowers, which are either heather of a proper size, unlike the giant stuff on the lower slopes, or "everlasting flowers", dry and papery compositæ which returning mountaineers wear in their hats to show they've done the climb. The flowers are just large daisies that don't die—they just fade away and disintegrate after a few months. The fellow in the white trousers looks spiky—I can't think why. The fellow in the white shorts looks frozen—reason obvious. The fellow on the far right probably has blisters. If that mist comes any lower, we're going to be on our hands and knees looking for footprints.

Here we are, still outward bound, at about 10,000 feet, resting for ten minutes and obviously in need of it. Henry looks as if he has gone to sleep standing up. The more energetic ones have dropped their packs: most of us have just dropped with our packs. A barren place, no need to ask where all the flowers have gone, they have deserted us some miles back. There is no sign of our faithful companion, the

ugly, tick-ridden, battleship-grey, mongrel bitch, who followed us from base up to about 11,000 feet, despite all our attempts to discourage her, including stories of dog-eating wizards who dwelt in the caves of Kilimanjaro. Fortunately she transferred her affections to Don and his party whom we met just below the hut, returning from their attempt on the summit. Beyond the ridge in the picture is another ridge, and beyond that is another, and beyond that...

A Postscript

Six months later I led a party of young people up Kilimanjaro, using my experience of the first climb. I was asked to do so by Major Wellesley Devitt, M.C., who was minister in charge of the Africa Inland Mission at Kijabe in Rift Valley Province. His fifteen year old daughter, Helen, was one of the party, with two of her girl friends from the American School at Kijabe; the rest was made up of American and African High School students at the Mission. We were based at the Mission at Loitokitok, and did very little preparation for the climb: youth and enthusiasm proved to be all that was needed. We followed the same route as before, sleeping in the two caves and in the hut, and carrying all our own equipment. We were properly shod and found the going not too difficult underfoot. The only problem we faced was the intense cold when we left the hut at three o'clock in the morning. Later another problem came to light: I had restricted rations on the climb in the interest of reducing weight, and some of the older boys, being normally steady eaters, felt hungry, but were too polite to tell me so. I heard about it

The Mission Party ready to go

through a third party later. But we all made it to the top and down again.

The Mission Party in the second cave

In the picture on the right appears, far right, a friend of mine from Kitui, District Officer Ian Buist, who unknown to me had climbed from the Tanganyika side of the mountain and had been as surprised as I was to find us both at the hut at the same time.

The Mission Party at the hut – final pitch tomorrow!

Later I was asked if I would help lead the second Outward Bound Course on the mountain, but I was due to go on leave to England, so had to decline the invitation. A year later I left Kenya for good, and I never achieved my third ascent of Kilimanjaro.

Word-List

A VOCABULARY OF SWAHILI WORDS CURRENT IN ENGLISH COLLOQUIAL SPEECH IN KENYA IN 1956.

Akili – Lit: intelligence. Arabic

Native rather than acquired – corresponds very closely to "common sense".

"These fellows will never learn anything – they just haven't the akili."
"For Heaven's sake, man, use a bit of akili!"

Askari – An African uniformed police constable. Arabic

Not used with reference to officers, whether African or European.

"The patrol consisted of a European Chief Inspector, an African Inspector and five askaris."

Bado – lit: not yet Arabic

Conveniently used to mean "soon", expressive of the intention to do something when the time is ripe, and meanwhile enjoining patience in the enquirer.

Bado kidogo – "in a little while", a variant, expressing the intention of doing something before the enquirer gets bored and goes away.

"Have you written that report yet?" "Bado."
"Daddy, will you mend my bicycle now?" "What's that? Oh, bado kidogo."

Banda – An open shed built of poles with low walls if any, (usually in mud and wattle) and usually a thatched roof. It is commonly used as a barn or as a temporary (or permanent) school classroom.

Baraza – lit: a verandah. Arabic

A meeting at which Africans are addressed by an administrative officer, so called because the original venue of such talks would have been the verandah of the latter's bungalow or office or tent. The word was traditionally used of such discussions on the verandahs of Zanzibar Arab merchants.

Bas – lit: the end. Hindi

Enough; finis; when (i.e., "that is enough soda.")

"Say when…" "Bas!"

Bibi – Originally the title given to a married lady among the Arabs. Hindi
An African's wife.

"Well, this African was riding along, carrying his bibi on the crossbar…"

Boi – lit: a servant. This has a plural maboi in Swahili, giving it status as a native African word, but usually treated as if it were the English word "boy", and spelt thus. As a term of reference it is often qualified by another noun, as in "house boy" or "shamba boy". As a form of address or summons it is capable of being uttered in a wide variety of tones, inclining to the peremptory. It is now (1956) officially discouraged because of its pejorative association with the homophonous English word.

Boma – lit: a fence surrounding a homestead or cattle-pen. Bantu

The area in a township, originally walled or fenced, embracing the administrative and other Government offices, together with a high proportion of the houses of the European officers. Used figuratively the word implies the corporate European life in a township in an African area.

"The mission at Mulango is about six miles from Kitui boma."
"It's a very friendly boma at Fort Hall."

Bundu – The bush, or wild country, including the forest, which supports the wildlife of the colony: uncultivated land, untouched by the tentacles of husbandry or civilisation. A Bantu word from further south in the continent. (Note – there is forest but no jungle in Africa.)

"When I came out here in 1904, I had to cut myself a farm out of the bundu."
"The police post is 'way out in the bundu – miles from anywhere."
"The new office boy's hopeless – fresh from the bundu, judging from what he appears to know."

Bundu-whacking – driving a vehicle across the plains or through the bush ignoring ready-made roads or tracks (if any).

Bunduki – a rifle or shotgun, often antiquated, so referred to however only when in the hands of an African.   Arabic – bunduk

Bure – lit: free; or as an adverb, gratuitously, fruitlessly   Possibly Arabic

The derived meaning is "without value", "utterly useless". It is used particularly of tools or machines.

"For God's sake don't touch the light switch! The whole electrical system's completely bure."
"This battery's bure kabisa (q.v.), and I've only had it a couple of months."

Chai – Tea. Only used to refer to tea prepared for drinking, a "cup of chai"; the dry commodity is referred to as "tea". Many Africans speaking English ask logically for "tea leaves" when buying the stuff.   Arabic

"Come on in and have a cup of chai!"
"Thanks, I could do with a cup of chai just now."

Chakula – food   Bantu

In very common use – used for prepared or cooked food, reflecting its literal meaning, "(something) to eat".

"Why not come and have some chakula with us tomorrow night."
"I think it's about time we knocked off for a spot of chakula."

Choo – (rhymes with "snow") = lit: – excrement.   Bantu, current in Zanzibar

A lavatory, ranging in quality from the earth closet or "long drop" to the very latest in Staffordshire enamel ware. Widely used euphemistically and a bit of a godsend at a time when the now popular English term "loo" had not yet been invented.

"The choo's at the end of the corridor, old man."

Dawa – medicine, in liquid, solid, powder or gaseous form, capable of being administered to man, beast or machine.

"But Mummy, I hate that dawa – it's awful!"
"The doctor's given me some ghastly-looking dawa this time."
"What sort of dawa do you think I should give my pigs?"
"Couldn't get the damn' car to go properly – then old Luigi squirted some dawa into the cylinders and she went as sweet as a bird."

Debe – the ubiquitous four-gallon paraffin tin, whose widespread use for carrying, for seating, and, when cut open and flattened, for roofing, ensured a wide currency to the term.   Hindi

Desturi – custom

"I'm sorry, old boy, I don't know what you used to do in Naivasha, but that's not the desturi round here."

Dobi – the week's washing (or the day's washing, since it is a daily chore of the houseboy). The original Hindi term for a washerman has been transferred to the object of his ministrations, there being no functionary in Kenya comparable to the dobi-wallah.

"My boy does the dobi three times a week."
Lately – "I do all my own dobi in the washing machine."

Dudu – any small creature, not always biologically an insect, large enough to excite attention or noxious enough to cause illness: not large enough or familiar enough to warrant a distinctive name, but small enough to crawl around one's neck and disappear inside one's shirt/blouse.   Bantu 'mdudu'

"Peter's still very poorly. He picked up some dudu on sarafi."
"There's a dudu in my soup (porridge, cabbage, hair, eye, etc.)"
"Some great dudu flew right into the lamp and landed in my whisky and soda."

Duka – a shop or stall, primarily the stone-walled, corrugated iron-roofed structure owned by African or Indian traders, often displaying its goods in a haphazard manner, although the name attaches also to the large general stores owned by Asians in the smaller townships.   Arabic

"I hear the Aga Khan's opening Jan Mohammed's new duka next month."
"I'm just popping down to the duka for some beer (onions, cigarettes, elastic bands, exercise, etc.)."

Fitina – lit: discord, antagonism, quarrelling. A mutual dislike giving rise to bad blood between neighbours or neighbouring social groups, regarded as totally irrational by the outside observer. This irrationality limits the use of the term to the objective observer: it is never used by the parties involved to describe their own attitudes.   Arabic

"You'll be very lucky to find a boma where there's no fitina."
"Most of the chief's time is taken up in settling land disputes; and these are usually the expression of local fitina."

Fundi – a craftsman in any branch of handicraft, although used most frequently in a restrictive sense for an expert in the building trades, whether a master builder or a bricklayer or a carpenter and joiner, or a worker in a subsidiary trade. Generally the craft is to be understood through the context, and may be used to refer to an expert in any field, especially languages.

"I'm taking my shoes to the fundi tomorrow to have them repaired."
"I paid a fundi twenty shillings to put up these shelves."
"I'm going to get a fundi to mend the fence tomorrow."
"The District Commissioner's a great fundi at Swahili (native law, growing sweet peas, etc.)."

Gari – a vehicle, often disreputable, or functional rather than decorative, e.g., a Land-Rover, lorry, pick-up, etc., less often a saloon.   Hindi

"I'm just taking the gari down to the garage to have the bumper put back on."
"Jump in the gari. Mind the bit of iron sticking up."
"Can you lay on a gari to take the football team to Ikutha on Saturday?"

Gombe – see Ng'ombe

Habari – news. Used as straight replacement of the English word.

"Any habari from Nairobi yet?"

Hapana – lit: "there is not any", used as the English "No" as a result of its being the answer in Swahili to the question "Is there any?". Capable of carrying a wide range of tones, replacing such phrases as "Of course not" and "Not on your life" as well as plain "no".   Bantu

"But don't you think he'll cotton on to the job eventually?" "Hapana! The fellow just hasn't got the akili. He'll always make a mess of things."
"Daddy, can't I have a new bike?" "Hapana!"
"And do you think I could make him see it? Hapana!"

Hivi-hivi – lit: this way, that way. In a haphazard manner.   Bantu

"That fellow's no fundi. He's put the garage up all hivi-hivi. The roof sags and the poles are at all angles."

Hodi – the traditional request for admission to a house in a country poor in knockers or doorbells. The correct Swahili reply of "Karibu" – "Come in" is usually set aside in favour of yelps or bellows of welcome from the inhabitants.   Arabic

Jembe – a traditional African hoe.

Kabisa – lit: completely, utterly, altogether. Used as an intensive in combination with other vernacular adjectives – bure kabisa, shinda'd kabisa, safi kabisa.

Kali – fierce. Used of a dog, an employer, a teacher, etc., and also of highly spiced food.

"George's new dog is very kali – it nearly had my hand off when I went to pat the brute."
"Our new teacher is very kali". (Clearly not a compliment.)
"This curry's very kali! What on earth did you put in it?"

Kanzu – the white overall coat worn by African house servants and common wear among Arabs on the coast.   Bantu

Karani – an African clerk in any office.   Arabic

Kazi – work.

"Sorry! I can't play golf tomorrow – too much kazi." (I.e., I have too much work to do.)
"The kazi in this job is practically killing me!"

Kesho – tomorrow. Its use brings to mind the Spanish "mañana", but procrastination is no great fault in the Kenya citizen. Nevertheless, it may be significant that the word for "yesterday", "juzi", is not widely used or even known.

"When are you going to clear up all this mess?" "Oh, kesho."

Kikapu – a woven basket, hand made locally, circular at the top and tapering almost to a point at the bottom, widely used by housewives of all races for carrying home the shopping. Bantu, current in Zanzibar.

Kikoi – a length of cloth used by Africans in place of trousers in some districts, especially near the coast, and also worn by women. The men wrap the cloth round their waist in the manner of a sarong, while the women wear it wrapped round their whole bodies.   Bantu, used in Zanzibar for cloth with a coloured border.

Kelele – a din, uproar or loud noise, produced orally or mechanically.   Bantu

"What was all that kelele about?" "Oh, just the usual argument about whose job it was to clean the outside of the windows."
"The crowd was kicking up a tremendous kelele."
"Drums, whistles, screams – just one hell of a kelele."

Kinanda – any musical instrument, including all stringed instruments, plus the mouth-organ and the piano accordion.   Bantu

"Come on, Jimmy, give us a tune on your kinanda!"

Kodi – the African poll tax.

Kofia – a hat, lid, etc.   Arabic

"That's a very maradadi kofia you're wearing."
"Now if you look closely you'll see that this tube has got a little kofia. Just unscrew that and squeeze, and out comes the tooth-paste."

Kuku – a chicken, usually the native breed of fowl with a distinctively naked neck.   Bantu

"It was a typical African hut, swarming with totos and kukus."
"We've got a very choice kuku for lunch."

Kuni – firewood, usually supplied as unsplit boughs about nine inches thick and four feet long.

Lakini – "but..." used with great emphasis and solemnity after all the points in favour of a project or asseveration have been made, to warn that there exists at least one insuperable obstacle or unanswerable objection.   Arabic (walakini)

"Ah, yes, that's perfectly true, and normally I should be willing to back you up to the hilt... lakini!... you just can't grow coffee in this part of the world!"

Mabati – corrugated iron: "A mabati roof."   Bantu

Mahindi – maize, usually on the cob.   Bantu

Maneno – lit. words, thence discussion, argument, debate. Any unnecessary words or fuss, any argument, any futile discussion on a point which is self-evident and thus closed to debate.

"Now let's see if we can't settle this business without a lot of maneno."
"There's a lot of maneno at these barazas – all the traditional quarrels are aired."
"Now then, what's all the maneno about?"

Mara moja – lit. one time, at once. Forthwith, without argument. The phrase lends itself to splitting, and a short English word, such as "bloody", is often inserted, the expanded phrase adding considerable weight to the command given.   Bantu

"Tell Kamau to bring last year's Official Gazettes, mara moja! (mara bloody moja!)"
"Timothy, five gin and tonics, mara moja!"

Maradadi – any decoration, frills or frippery: anything regarded as not purely functional. Used both as substantive and adjective, sometimes as slightly derogatory, sometimes to express admiration, grudging or otherwise.

"What's the idea of the fancy border on this notice board?" "Oh, I thought a bit of maradadi would look nice."
"Mummy, I want a big birthday cake with lots of maradadi icing."
"I say, I like your tie! Very maradadi with that fringe!"

Mingi – much, a lot. May be used as a substantive, adjective or adverb.   Bantu

"Mummy, I want some more milk on my corn flakes." "But darling, you already have some." "I know, Mummy, but I want mingi."
"Come home soon, darling, I miss you mingi, mingi, mingi."

Mpishi – a cook.

Mtoto – commonly "toto". An African child. The plural is "watoto" but in European usage "totos".
                                            Bantu

Mzee – an old man. Used as a polite form of address to an elderly African, or in referring to him.
                                            Bantu

"Don't worry about your gari, old man. I'll get the mzee to clean it for you tomorrow."

Ng'ombe – an African cow, of indeterminate, mongrel breed. Commonly "gombe", plural "gombes".   Bantu

Nusu-nusu – half and half, used widely to indicate the ideal proportions of whisky and soda.
                                            Arabic

"How would you like it, old boy?" "Oh, nusu-nusu."

Nyapara – an African headman or overseer on a European farm. "Mnyapara" was the title given to the head of a caravan or expedition or army.   Bantu

Panga – the long-bladed cutting tool of the African labourer, in size and shape resembling when straight the machete and when curved the scimitar. Used for a very wide variety of purposes, from digging post-holes to murder. Bantu 'upanga'

Piga – the root of a verb meaning "to beat", used in the form "piga'd" to mean defeated or beaten in a figurative sense. Bantu

"This problem's got me piga'd."

Polepole – slowly; softly, softly; carefully. Rhymes with "roly-poly". In wide use. Bantu

"I say, careful, old man, take it polepole!"
"Now we've got to go very polepole in this matter."

Posho – ground maize flour. Originally the word meant just "rations" but later came to signify the staple food of which the wages of the soldier or labourer in part consisted. Bantu

Rafiki – a friend.

Safari – a journey, usually extended over a period of two days or more, undertaken by a hunting party or a government official. Arabic

"Is the District Commissioner in?" "No, he's on safari this week." (I.e. he is making a tour of inspection of the District.)

Safi – clean, of great purity. Often used of language.

"You should hear the new District Officer speaking Swahili. Very safi."

Shamba – a garden.

1. The plot of land, consolidated or fragmented, owned or occupied by an African.
2. The vegetable garden of a European farmer or householder.
3. A plantation of any kind.

Shauri – a heated discussion or the expression of a grievance, usually very vehement and requiring for its settlement the arbitration of a third party. The settlement of such local disputes in an African area is an important part of the duties of an Administrative officer, acting in an advisory or judicial capacity. Also used in the phrase "It's his shauri", that is, "He is the man responsible for the matter in question." Bantu

"You two look very fierce – what's the shauri?"
"There's going to be one hell of a shauri when the D.C. gets to hear about this."
"Look, laddie, this isn't anything to do with me. Go and ask Bill Hawkins – it's his shauri."

Shenzi – uncivilised, used particularly to describe poor workmanship, a native breed of dog, or unspeakable conduct. Derived from "kishenzi", an uncivilised African. Bantu

"That's a most peculiar-looking dog you've got there." "Oh, that's not mine – it's just a shenzi that keeps following me about."
"Do you mean to say he's left his wife and gone off with that young Clifford girl? Now that's what I call shenzi behaviour."
"That's a shenzi-looking chair. It looks as if it would collapse if anyone sat on it."

Shinda – used in the form "shinda'd" in the same way as "piga'd". Used figuratively to denote the inability to solve a problem, or to carry out a declared intention, such as to grow decent roses in the tropics. Bantu

"Well, I can't make head or tail of this. I'm shinda'd kabisa."

Silanga – a dam, usually a sub-surface dam in which the river behind the dam is allowed to fill with sand or silt so as to slow evaporation. The knowledge of and use of the term seems to be confined to Agricultural Officers working in African areas and concerned with water conservation and the damming of rivers and water catchment areas.

Simi – the short native sword, which neither boasts nor deserves any loftier name.   Bantu

Sufuria – a round shallow broad-rimmed cooking pot, made of any light metal in a wide variety of sizes and sold by weight: in universal use among all households in the lower income brackets.

Taka-taka – dirt, rubbish, mess: anything which makes the place look untidy, at times used unkindly of persons.   Bantu

"My dear, the boy just sweeps all the taka-taka under the mat."
"Oh, I know that family! A load of taka-taka the lot of them."

Tembo – the native brewed beer, highly popular among Africans but not always hygienically prepared.   Bantu

Toto – see "mtoto".

Wadudu – plural of "mdudu".

Wapi – lit. which place? Used in place of "Where?" In Swahili the word always follows the noun or verb to which it refers, but in English usage it is promoted to the position normally occupied by "Where?" when the latter word is used as an interrogative to enquire only after the whereabouts of objects.   Bantu

"Wapi my (bloody) cuff-links/car key/blotting paper/green and yellow check socks?"